THE FEELING-STATE THEORY & PROTOCOLS

FOR

BEHAVIORAL AND SUBSTANCE ADDICTIONS

A Breakthrough in the Treatment of Addictions, Compulsions, Obsessions, Codependence, and Anger

Robert Miller, PhD

ImTT Press
Del Mar, CA

THE FEELING-STATE THEORY & PROTOCOLS

Robert Miller, PhD

ImTT Press, publisher

Acknowledgements

Feeling-State Therapy has been shaped over many years
by the feedback and experiences of my clients and therapists
who have used this approach. I would like to thank them for their
criticism and their support. Both were necessary.

I would also like to especially thank Dr. Francine Shapiro
for her amazing contribution to psychological treatment.
Her work formed the original foundation for the development
of the Feeling-State Theory and protocols.

I am deeply grateful for all she has accomplished.

C

ImTT Press, publisher

E

People say what we're all seeking is a meaning for life.

I don't think that's what we're really seeking.

I think that what we're really seeking is an experience of being alive,

so that our life experiences on the purely physical plane

will have resonance within our innermost being and reality,

so that we actually feel the rapture of being alive in our bodies.

(Joseph Campbell, 1991, in *The Power of Myth*)..

E

ImTT Press, publisher

Table of Contents

ImTT Press, publisher

Introduction

My first insight leading to Feeling-State Therapy occurred when I had been working on my own food issues. A year previously, I had decided to not control my eating but to resolve the problem. Nothing had worked. Lying down on my bed, somewhat in despair, I asked myself what I felt when I was eating brownies. Imagining myself in the moment of eating a brownie, what I experienced was an intense excitement. After breaking the link between the feeling of excitement and brownies, I no longer felt any desire to eat a brownie. That experience led me to work with a client who had eating issues and another who had a shopping compulsion. After helping them successfully resolving those issues, I knew I had something. I was so excited I couldn't sleep for three days.

Over time, Feeling-State Theory and the treatment protocols have continued to develop. The basic understanding of what causes compulsions and addictions has stayed the same, but I have refined the application of the theory and understanding of how to identify feeling-states.

Behavioral and substance addictions result from one of two different psychological dynamics—both of which can exist within the same person: seeking a positive feeling and avoiding a negative feeling. Feeling-State Therapy focuses on the dynamic of the seeking of the positive feeling such as is seen in the "chasing the dragon" behavior of heroin addicts.

This book explains the cause and treatment for behavioral and substance addictions, as well as many other behaviors that, surprisingly, turned out to have feeling-states motivating the behavior. Feeling-State Therapy has ended the "nightmare" for what is now thousands of people that the addictive/compulsive behavior created in their lives.

ImTT Press, publisher

ImTT Press, publisher

Chapter 1

The Feeling-State Theory of Behavioral and Substance Addictions

Feeling-State Therapy (FST) is a break-through in the treatment of behavioral and substance addictions that eliminates a powerful psychological dynamic creating addictive/compulsive behavior. Energized by survival needs, normal healthy desires, linked with behavior, undermines survival. Feeling-State Theory explains how this dynamic is created and how to break the linkage between survival needs and behavior.

Currently, many forms of treatment require some form of willpower to maintain sobriety. Clearly, willpower often fails to prevent the person from doing the behavior. Even when a person quits doing one behavior, another behavior may take its place. The mental struggle to maintain sobriety is exhausting; willpower can only last so long. Fighting against your own survival needs is an uphill battle.

The dilemma that a person with an addiction/compulsion faces is:

Do the behavior and get the intensely desired feeling including the negative consequences of that behavior;

or

Not Do the behavior, not have the negative consequences, but also not get the desperately wanted feeling.

FS treatment <u>solves</u> this dilemma by breaking the fixated linkage between the feeling and the behavior. Breaking this linkage means that the intensely desired feeling is no longer energizing the behavior. Once the linkage is broken, there is no need to exercise willpower in order to stop performing the behavior; there is no compulsion to overcome. The person is then free to experience that feeling as part of a healthy, natural behavior.

ImTT Press, publisher

Feeling-State Theory examines how these intense linkages between survival feelings and behavior are formed and explains how to break the linkages—breaking the links of the chains that destroy lives. Therapists who utilize FS treatment have helped many people overcome behavior that has had a negative effect on their lives.

In addition to behavioral and substance addictions, many of the most difficult-to-treat behaviors—such as codependence, anger, and certain types of obsessions—are also the result of a desired feeling linked with a behavior.

The Feeling-State Theory has been previously described in articles published in the journal *Traumatology (2010)* and the *Journal of EMDR Research and Practice (2012)*. The protocol for eliminating addiction described in those articles is called the Feeling-State Addiction Protocol (FSAP). The FSAP utilizes a modified form of Eye Movement Desensitization and Reprocessing (EMDR) to process the feeling-states.

The Feeling-State model of compulsive and addictive behaviors focuses on identifying and resolving the powerful psychological dynamic that creates these behaviors. The basic concept is simple: an intensely desired feeling becomes fixated with a behavior. Once the feeling is fixated with the behavior, whenever the person wants to experience the feeling, he performs the behavior, even though the person may not be aware of the feeling linked with the behavior.

Alice had a shopping compulsion. She would shop at expensive "elite" stores and buy some item that was more than she could afford, like a $500 belt. Alice had an FS linking the behavior of buying clothes at expensive stores with the feeling that she was "special"—that she was part of the elite group of people who could afford to buy clothes at those stores. Whenever Alice felt the desire to feel "special," she would experience an urge or craving to shop. Once the linkage between the feeling of being "special" and the behavior of buying expensive clothes was broken, Alice no longer had any urges or cravings to buy expensive clothes she couldn't afford.

Alice's story illustrates the basics of the Feeling-State model of treatment for compulsions and addictions. Processing an addiction requires two steps:

1. Identification of the positive feeling fixated with the behavior, and

2. Breaking the fixation between the feeling and behavior, which releases the person from the compulsion to perform that behavior.

The concept is simple—the challenge is in the identification of the feeling.

ImTT Press, publisher

Feeling-State Theory

The Feeling-State Theory of Behavioral and Substance Addictions postulates that addictions (both behavioral and substance) are created when positive feelings become rigidly linked with specific objects, a person, or a behavior. The concept of a unit consisting of a <u>positive feeling</u> linked with a <u>behavior</u> is called a "feeling-state" (FS).

When a feeling-state is activated, the entire psycho-physiological pattern is activated. The activation of the pattern then activates the out-of-control behavior. For Alice in the above example, the feeling-state was composed of the feeling of being "special" that was fixated with the behavior of buying expensive clothes. Once activated, Alice bought clothes she couldn't afford.

An example of a drug addiction related to an FS is Rick's marijuana addiction. Rick began smoking marijuana in high school with a group of his friends. They would get together after school, talk about different "guy" things, and smoke marijuana. Rick identified the feeling of "fitting in" or belonging that he experienced during those times. So Rick's marijuana craving was the result of his desire to feel that he "belonged" that had become fixated with smoking marijuana.

FSs do not change or adapt with experience.

When Jeri won a large amount of money playing Texas Hold'em, the feeling of winning was so intense that the <u>positive feeling of "winning"</u> became fixated, in his mind, with the <u>behavior of playing Texas Hold'em.</u> That fixated "winning" memory was not altered in any way by his steadily losing large amounts of money over the next several years after the "winning" fixation was created. Once the FS was created, no amount of negative "losing" experiences would change or affect that memory of winning.

If Jeri's experience had not created an FS, he would have stopped playing after the pain of his losing overwhelmed the excitement of his memory of winning. However, Jeri's pain of losing was overridden by his fixated memory of winning. Jeri's experience illustrates the following truth about feeling-states:

The FS remains unchanged, unaffected by cognitive insights or negative experiences. The FS is preserved in its original form, no matter what disastrous results flow from the behavior embedded within it.

The fixation of the memory (the FS) is the reason that addictive behavior has been so difficult to control. Embedded in the FS is an intensely desired feeling (Jeri's desire to feel like a winner). If the person stops doing the behavior, he also stops getting the intensely desired feeling. Asking a person to give up that behavior is the same as asking them to give up that powerfully desired feeling. As long as the behavior is linked with the feeling, the urge to do that behavior will be intensely powerful—as powerful as the intensity of the person's desire to experience the feeling. Even when a person has decided that the consequences of the behavior are so destructive that he has to stop, he is still in a fight with his own intense desires. No wonder relapse is the norm.

The "Feeling"

In Feeling-State Theory, the "feeling" must meet two requirements to qualify as a feeling embedded in the FS:

1. The identified feeling is always self-referential. In other words, the "feeling" is always about the self. "I feel I am special," "I feel I am powerful," and "I feel I belong" are statements that express what a person feels about himself in regards to a person, object, or behavior. In the Feeling-State model, the feeling embedded in the FS is never about the other person or behavior.

2. The FS-feeling is an "assured survival feeling" (ASF). ASFs are the result of experiences that promote a person's survival. Examples of ASFs are feelings of belonging, being special, important, loved, or safe. (ASFs will be discussed further in the chapter on feeling-states.) The goal of the FS treatment is to de-link the embedded ASF from the behavior so that the person can be released from the compulsion of doing that behavior.

In this book, for ease of reading, I will usually discuss the ASF as linked with a behavior. However, the ASF can be linked with a behavior, a specific person, or an object.

Definitions:

Feeling in FS = Assured-Survival Feeling (ASF)

Feeling-State = Fixation of ASF with a Behavior, Person, or Object

---

Feeling-State Treatment

Breaks the fixated link between the desired ASF and the behavior, which eliminates the FS-caused addictive/compulsive behavior.

ImTT Press, publisher

ASFs and Feeling-States

Any ASF can be linked with any behavior

In the Feeling-State Theory, there is no predictive relationship between any specific ASF with any specific behavior. Any ASF can be linked with any behavior.

John's, Tim's, and Dustin's compulsions are good examples showing that any ASF can be linked with any behavior, no matter how unrelated to the behavior the feeling may appear to be.

John: John had a gambling problem. After losing over a million dollars in ten years, he still could not stop playing poker. John had been a non-compulsive gambler until he won a lot of money in one poker hand. From that point, his gambling was out of control. For John, the feeling-state was composed of the feeling of being a "winner" combined with the behavior of playing poker.

Tim: Tim, however, had a completely different feeling associated with playing poker. What Tim wanted was the feeling of connection with his father. When Tim was growing up, he watched his father playing poker with the "guys." He longed to be part of the group so that he could be with his father. The longed-for event finally occurred when he was in college. The result was that, when Tim played poker, he felt bonded with his father. For Tim, the feeling-state was composed of the feeling of "connection with his father" combined with the behavior of playing poker.

Dustin: Dustin's sexual compulsion began in high school. He and three other buddies set up a competition to see who could have sex with the greatest number of women. This game became widely known among the other kids at school, and they wagered bets on who would be the winner. The outcome was close, but Dustin won the competition.

He described his feeling of "winning" as being the "Big Man on Campus" (BMC), which felt as if he were experiencing "the best orgasm I have ever had." For Dustin, the feeling-state was composed of the feeling of "winning" (being BMC) combined with the behavior of having sex with as many women as he could and reporting it to his friends at which point he received their acknowledgment of his "victory."

John: FS = "Winning" + Poker

Tim: FS = "Father Connection" + Poker

Dustin: FS = "Winning" (BMC)
+ Telling Buddy of Sexual Conquest

The examples of John and Tim illustrate how the same behavior (playing poker) can be fixated with different feelings. John's gambling was connected with a winning feeling, while Tim's gambling was connected with a bonding feeling. On the other hand, the same feeling (winning) can be connected with different behaviors. John experienced winning through playing poker; Dustin experienced winning (being BMC) by being acknowledged for having had sex with the greatest number of women. A fundamental premise of Feeling-State Theory, therefore, is that *any ASF can become fixated with any behavior.*

Creation of a Feeling-State

Feeling-states are created when intensified ASFs are experienced while doing some behavior, any behavior. The behavior could be gambling, shopping, driving, sex—or really, any behavior. The intensity of the feeling while doing the behavior creates the feeling-state—linking the feeling with the behavior. The type of behavior is irrelevant. That is why there are so many different kinds of addictions.

A person can become addicted or feel a compulsion to perform any behavior if the behavior occurs while the person experiences an intensified ASF.

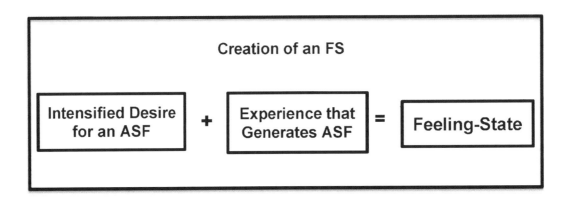

Once the feeling-state is formed, then any kind of activating event that induces the need for the desired feeling will result in the person feeling the compulsion to perform the behavior in order to experience the desired feeling linked with it.

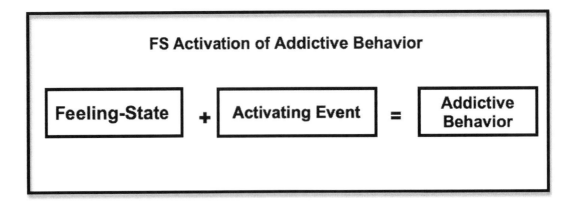

For example, Dustin's sexual compulsion illustrates how an FS can be created. Dustin's behavior involved seducing women and then bragging to one of his male friends about his "victory." Once his friend acknowledged Dustin's sexual conquest, he would have to find another woman to seduce so that he could experience another "victory."

Dustin's sexual compulsion began in high school when he and his friends decided to have a contest to see who could have sex with the greatest number of women. Dustin won and experienced an intense feeling of being, in Dustin's words, the "Big Man on Campus" (BMC).

The BMC is an ASF because the feeling was an acknowledgment of having attained high status within his group. As a result, an FS was created that linked the acknowledgment for his sexual conquest with the feeling of being the "Big Man on Campus."

This intense experience of being the "Big Man on Campus" created an FS that preserved his age-related behavior linked with the desired feeling of being high status ("BMC"). In other words, Dustin's behavior at 35 years old was the result of the feeling-state that had been created so long ago in high school.

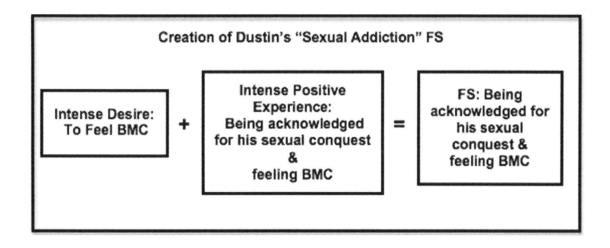

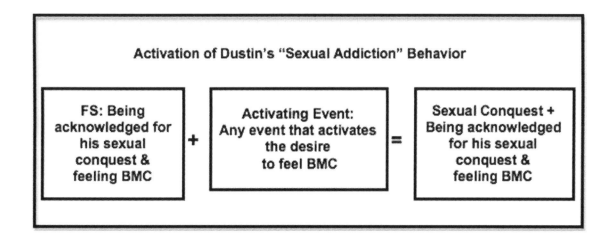

The Creation of Feeling-States

The biological drive to live is the motivation underlying the feelings embedded in a feeling-state. For example, whether the feeling is a feeling of belonging, importance, feeling special, or feeling safe, the feeling derives its power from the irrepressible desire to live. That is why addictions have been so difficult to resolve. As long as the survival motivated feelings are linked with the behavior, then as far as the "addicted" person is concerned, stopping the behavior means the person will not obtain the feeling that assures the person that his survival needs will be met.

An example of a feeling linked with survival needs is the feeling of "belonging." Human beings can only exist within a community. As we develop from being infants to children, and later as adults, we require other people to help us meet our basic survival needs of food, clothing, and shelter, as well as many other non-material needs. Experiences that make us feel that we "belong" assure us that our specific survival needs will be meet.

When our experiences do not provide that feeling of "belonging," the biological need for survival intensifies our need for a "belonging" experience that would provide a feeling that, at least for the moment, we need not worry because our survival is assured. The consequence of that intensified need for the "belonging" experience is the creation of a feeling-state with the feeling of "belonging" fixated with a behavior—any behavior, so long as the person experiences the feeling of "belonging" at the time when performing the behavior.

All FSs are created by the same basic psychological dynamic. A person who does not have ongoing experiences that generate the feeling that his survival is assured will have an intensified need for experiences that produce that feeling. When the person does obtain that needed experience, the intensified need fixates the feeling with the behavior, object, or person that happened to be part of the experience.

From that point on, the person obtains that assured-survival feeling by re-creating the experience with the behavior, object, or person. The fixation is so intense that, even when the consequences of the behavior threaten current survival, the fixation does not change and the behavior does not adapt with experience.

While the desire to live usually manifests in the motivation to meet basic survival needs, the desire to live also manifests in the desire to feel alive. Even when physical survival is threatened by the behavior, the desire to feel alive can motivate people to risk their physical survival. The euphoria-producing experiences of certain drugs, the adrenaline-excitement of danger, and the intense creative/flow "zone" are experiences that make people feel intensely alive. The need to feel intensely alive is a powerful desire that, in its various forms, creates FSs.

The desires to survive, to live, and to feel intensely alive are the motivations behind all FSs. That is why addictive/compulsive types of behaviors have been so difficult to manage behaviorally. Without breaking the link between the assured-survival feeling and the behavior, managing the behavior means opposing the person's desire to live—more likely than not, a losing battle. Morality and "character" are weak weapons to do battle against the demands of the survival needs.

ImTT Press, publisher

Because the term "assured-survival feeling" (ASF) is not easily useful in therapy, the term "positive feelings" will often be used in this book. Asking a person to identify which "assured-survival feeling" is linked with his "smoking with his buddies" behavior is not likely to elicit a useful response. Therefore, the term "positive feeling" will be used instead. However, *the therapist must understand that the only type of positive feeling that is embedded in an FS is an assured-survival type of positive feeling.*

ASFs are divided into the following four categories: safety, relational, winning (status), and sensation-alive. Some ASFs, especially the ones expressed as phrases, may stimulate feelings in more than one category. For example, the ASF "bonding" may activate feelings related to both relational and safety issues. "Invincible" may include categories of safety, relational, and winning. For the purpose of treatment, processing the FS does not require distinguishing between these categories. However, Phase 4, processing of the underlying NC, may require a more nuanced understanding of the FS in order to identify the NC. A list of ASFs is in the Appendix.

Because only the assured-survival type of positive feeling is embedded in FSs, not all feelings that people will initially identify as the positive feeling linked with the behavior are actually the correct feeling. For example, people will often identify "comfort" or "relaxation" as a feeling they experience after smoking.

As will be explained later in the book (page 48), feelings of relaxation and/or comfort are not the feelings embedded in an FS. These feelings are not assured-survival feelings and are, therefore, not the feelings that are fixated with the behavior, object, or person. Only positive feelings that are ASFs are the feelings embedded in an FS.

<u>Assured-Survival Feelings (ASFs)</u> are the ONLY

<u>Positive Feelings</u> that create an FS

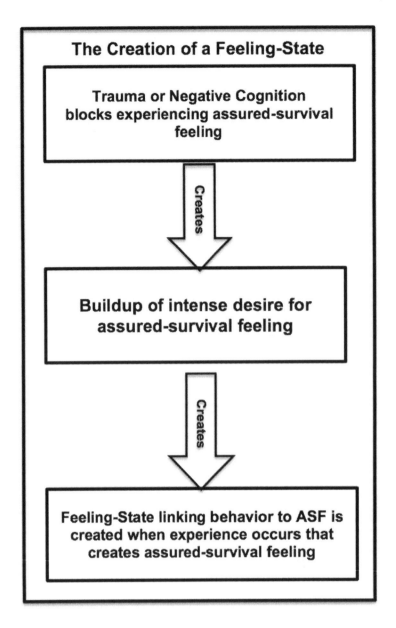

The Creation of a Feeling-State

Trauma or Negative Cognition
blocks experiencing assured-survival
feeling

Creates

Buildup of intense desire for
assured-survival feeling

Creates

Feeling-State linking behavior to ASF is
created when experience occurs that
creates assured-survival feeling

Sarah had an intense urge to reconnect with an abusive ex-boyfriend. Though she vigorously stated during therapy sessions that he was "bad" for her, Sarah struggled with her urge to get back together with him. Sometimes she lost the fight with herself.

Sarah's childhood was one of emotional deprivation. She reported that there was almost no physical loving contact or emotional connection with any member of her family. Sarah had worked on family issues in therapy. Focusing on her negative childhood experiences had no effect on her desire to be with her ex-boyfriend. Using a different approach, the author asked, "What's the most positive experience you have ever had with your boyfriend?"

Sarah described a time when he was holding her and she felt, for the first time in her life, an intense and wonderful feeling of "wholeness." Even though the event lasted only a few minutes, Sarah's feeling of "wholeness" had become linked with her boyfriend. The intensity of Sarah's desire for wholeness was similar to a starving person's reaction to food—the greater the hunger, the more intense the response. Sarah's emotional deprivation from childhood intensified Sarah's desire to feel "whole." When she experienced that feeling while being held by her boyfriend, the FS was created, linking the feeling of wholeness with her boyfriend.

10   ImTT Press, publisher

Breaking the link between the feeling of "wholeness" and the image of her "boyfriend" eliminated Sarah's urge to be with him.

Sarah had identified her assured-survival feeling as a feeling of "wholeness." Calling the feeling she was experiencing "wholeness" was Sarah's way of combining the feeling of belonging and safety. Separating the feeling into its component parts would not have been therapeutically necessary or useful.

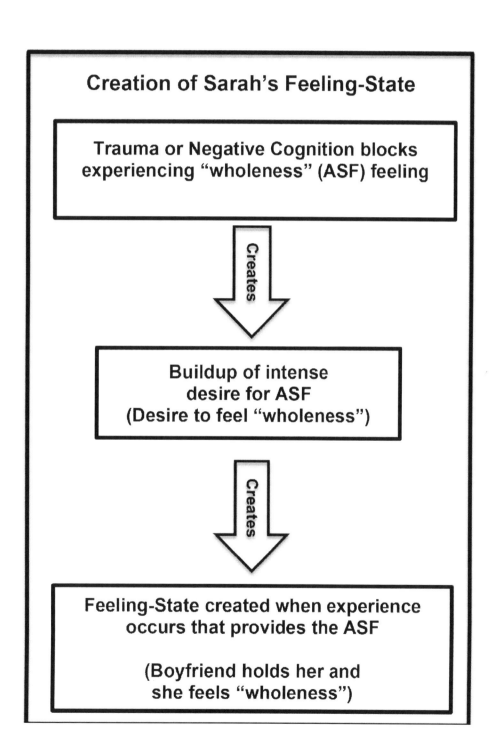

Creation of Sarah's Feeling-State

Trauma or Negative Cognition blocks experiencing "wholeness" (ASF) feeling

Creates

Buildup of intense desire for ASF (Desire to feel "wholeness")

Creates

Feeling-State created when experience occurs that provides the ASF

(Boyfriend holds her and she feels "wholeness")

"Creation of an Addiction" Flow Chart

The following flow chart entitled "'Creation of an Addiction' Flow Chart" illustrates how addictive behavior may be created

Step 1: Some form of abuse or neglect that creates a negative cognition about the self ("I'm a loser").

Step 2: The NC creates a blockage to obtaining the desired feeling (the desire to feel like a winner).

Step 3: Over time, the desire to experience the feeling grows in intensity.

Step 4: A positive event occurs in which the person intensely experiences the desired feeling (winning a large hand at poker), creating an FS.

Step 5: Addictive behavior (compulsive gambling) is performed when the FS is activated.

"Creation of an Addiction" Flow Chart

Trauma or neglect that creates negative cognition

Negative cognition blocks experiencing desired ASF

Buildup of intense desire for the desired ASF

Creation of the FS during an experience that generates the desired ASF

Addictive behavior

The Goal of Addictive/Compulsive Behavior is to Experience the ASF

The real but usually hidden goal of addictive/compulsive behavior is to experience the positive feeling linked with the behavior. In other words, the person performs the behavior only to experience the feeling linked with it.

For example, the real object of Dustin's sexual behavior was to feel that he was the "BMC"; engaging in sex was not the true object of his behavior. Sarah wanted to experience the feeling of "wholeness," not to reconnect with her abusive ex-boyfriend. Terri wanted to feel special, not to own clothes she did not even wear.

No matter what the compulsive behavior is, what the person really seeks is the feeling that is linked to that behavior.

The different types of behaviors that are often part of feeling-states include gambling, shopping, kleptomania, video-game playing, sex, pornography, socializing, and relationship "addictions."

Focusing treatment on what the person really desires—the feeling linked with the behavior and not the behavior itself—helps both the therapist and client focus on the psychological dynamic that actually created the behavior.

Behavior changes when the psychological dynamic motivating the behavior is eliminated.

The real goal of addictive/compulsive behavior is to experience the positive feeling (the ASF) linked with the behavior.

ImTT Press, publisher

The Real Need is for Healthy Feelings, Not Destructive Behaviors

An important premise of the Feeling-State Theory is that all the persistent and recurrent maladaptive behaviors associated with addictions have their basis in normal, healthy needs that are a normal part of everyone's psyche. The need to be successful, to belong, to win, for wholeness, et cetera, are all normal, healthy needs that are motivated by a desire to survive.

The distortion into persistent and recurrent maladaptive behavior occurs because a feeling related to that need (e.g., feeling successful) has become rigidly linked with a particular behavior and is no longer subject to rational control. The good news for treatment is that, once the feeling-state is broken, the person automatically begins to seek more appropriate ways to obtain the desired feeling.

Understanding that the real need is for healthy feelings—not destructive behaviors—is crucial for both therapist and client.

For the therapist, this viewpoint helps to avoid focusing on the behavior that may be disgusting or revolting to the therapist and, instead, focus on the natural, healthy desires of the client. If the client feels a negative reaction from the therapist, he will not feel safe to process the compulsion. Knowing that addictive/compulsive behaviors are linked with healthy, normal needs will make treatment for some particularly challenging behaviors less difficult for the therapist.

For the client, understanding that the feeling driving the behavior arises from a healthy, normal need reduces resistance to identifying the feeling. If the person believes that the feeling linked with the behavior might be discovered to be grotesque or horrible, he will naturally resist identifying the feeling. The person may already feel that something is horribly wrong with himself. Informing him that the feeling that he wants is a natural and healthy feeling will make identifying the feeling—and thus the therapy—easier because there will be less resistance to the process.

The real need is for <u>healthy</u> feelings–<u>NOT</u> destructive behaviors.

ImTT Press, publisher

Chapter 2

The Feeling-State Protocols

The processing of a feeling-state can be performed with either FSIP or the FSAP. The FSIP uses the Image De-Construction Protocol (IDP) of Image Transformation Therapy (ImTT), and the FSAP uses the bilateral stimulation (BLS) protocol of Eye Movement Desensitization and Reprocessing (EMDR). The processing of feeling-states was originally accomplished using the EMDR approach, but either approach can be used.

The articles published in the journals *Traumatolgy* (2010) and *Journal of EMDR Clinical Practice and Research* (2012) utilize the EMDR method.

There are two important similarities between the Feeling-State Image Protocol (FSIP) and the Feeling-State Addiction Protocol (FSAP).

1. The identification of the FS is the same in both protocols, and

2. An underlying negative memory or image is processed in Phase 4.

The FSIP and FSAP are different as follows:

1. The ImTT approach does not require the person to intensely experience the FS. The difference means that the FSIP is easier to use when targeting a high-intensity feeling that the client fears may cause relapse (see discussion pg. 52). Difficulty working with an intense FS can be avoided by utilizing the Euphoric Sensation Release Protocol to reduce the intensity of the FS.

2. Another difference between the FSIP and the FSAP is in the processing of the trauma in Phase 4. In EMDR treatment, the person has to experience the emotion or "ring the bell" in order to process the trauma. In stark contrast to the "re-experiencing" that is required for effective EMDR treatment, ImTT treatment of trauma does not require the person to experience the feeling. The person is specifically instructed to not experience the feeling during the release process. This approach minimizes flooding and dissociation, making the processing of trauma easier for the client and the therapist.

The ImTT treatment for trauma is described in *Image Transformation Therapy* (Miller, 2015).

The Feeling-State Image Protocol

The FSIP Flow Chart

The FSIP flow chart illustrates the different steps of the FSIP. The FSIP processes the addictive behavior in the reverse direction in which it was created.

Starting with the addictive behavior, the FSIP processes the FS first. Then the trauma or negative event that created the intense desire for the ASF is processed.

Processing the FS first before processing the trauma ensures that the negative cognition and trauma targeted for processing are directly related to the addiction.

People have many different negative cognitions and traumas. Discerning which trauma is related to the addiction before processing the FS would be both extremely difficult and unnecessary.

Processing the FS prior to processing the NC allows the underlying trauma to easily surface to awareness. In fact, sometimes the trauma begins to emerge before the FS is even completely processed.

ImTT Press, publisher

FSIP Flow Chart

Identify the addictive behavior

Identify the intensified ASF driving the behavior

Process the FS

(Created by the intensified ASF)

Identify the negative cognition (NC)

that blocks experiencing the ASF

Either float back to the event creating the NC or

create an image resonating with the NC

Process the negative memory or image

ImTT Press, publisher

The Feeling-State Image Protocol

The words in italics are a script for questions the therapist might ask the client.

Phase 1: History and Evaluation

1. Obtain history, frequency, and context of the addictive behavior.

2. Evaluate the person for having adequate coping skills to manage negative feelings if the person is no longer using substances to cope. If the person is too fragile for releasing the addictive behavior, process the pain, terror, and traumas until the person is capable of coping without the addictive behavior.

Phase 2: Preparation

3. Explain the FSIP including the Feeling-State Theory and how fixated memories cause behavioral and substance addictions.

4. Explain how addictive behavior can also be used to avoid memories and feelings.

5. Prepare the client for trauma processing by explaining Image Transformation Therapy and the link between trauma and feeling-states.

6. Release an emotional pain utilizing the P/TRP so that the person has an experience of the protocol and can understand the basic process.

Phase 3: Processing the FS

7. Identify the specific aspect of the addictive behavior that has the most intensity associated with it. If the addiction is to a stimulant drug, then the rush/euphoria memory is processed first. However, if some other memory is more intense, process that first. The starting memory may be the first time or the most recent—whichever is most potent.

8. Identify the specific self-referential positive feeling (ASF) linked with the addictive behavior.

9. Instruct the client to combine 1) visualizing, <u>as if from a distance</u>, doing the addictive behavior and 2) <u>lightly experiencing</u> the positive feeling.

10. Eliminate the image with the Image De-Construction Protocol.

11. If the ASF is a drug-induced Sensation-FS of rush or euphoria, release the reduced feeling-sensation using the Euphoric Sensation Release Protocol (ESRP). If the ASF is not a drug-induced Sensation-FS, go to step 14 without doing the ESRP.

12. After releasing the FS with the ESRP, obtain PFS level. If the PFS is greater than 1, either repeat the IDP or eliminate other Sensation-FSs related to the drug, as necessary, by repeating Steps 7-11.

ImTT Press, publisher

13. After eliminating the Sensation-FSs, use the Changing Patterns Protocol focusing on different events related to the FS.

14. Give homework to facilitate an evaluation of the progress of therapy and to elicit any other feelings related to the addictive behavior.

15. During the next session, reevaluate the addictive behavior for the feeling-state identified in the last session. If that FS is still active, continue processing. If the FS has been eliminated, evaluate for other FSs.

16. Steps 7—15 are performed again as necessary.

Phase 4: Process the NC and Image Underlying the FS

17. Identify the NC linked with the wanted feeling. (*What's the negative belief you have about yourself that makes you feel you can't belong? connect? aren't important? et cetera.*)

18. Identify the image or memory linked with the NC.
     (*Can you remember an event that made you feel that way?*)

19. Process the NC or memory/image with ImTT.

Phase 5: Process   Negative   Images   and   Cognitions   Caused   by   the   FS-created Behavior

20. Use memories or a fantasy to identify the negative image that was created as a result of the addictive behavior.

21. Process the image with ImTT. Intense feelings of guilt or shame may need to be processed first if there is resistance to releasing the image.

Phase 6: Process the Memories and Images that May Cause Anxiety about Relapsing

22. Identify the image or memories related to expectations or anxiety about relapsing.

23. Process the identified image or memory with ImTT.

Discussion of the FSIP

The FSIP establishes all the elements that must be processed in order to eliminate compulsive behavior resulting from a feeling-state. Because the FSs have such destructive and negative influences on a person's life, eliminating the addiction makes working through other issues easier; so treatment should stay focused on processing the FS even when other issues arise.

When processing the FS with the IDP, if the person begins to associate with traumatic memories and the person can be reasonably brought back to processing the FS, then the FSIP processing should be continued. However, if the traumatic memory is too overwhelming and must be immediately worked through, this is not a problem. Diverging from the protocol is common.

After working through the trauma, return to the point in the protocol where the divergence occurred and pick up where you left off with the FSIP processing. As long as all the elements of the protocol are done, the addictive behavior created by the FS will be eliminated. Divergences from the protocol are perfectly acceptable. The FS isn't going anywhere until it is processed.

Phase 1: Phase 1 has three purposes.

1. Safety: The first purpose is to establish the general safety of the client for removing FSs. Feeling-States are very powerful dynamics that can serve to emotionally stabilize a person. When an FS is eliminated, that source of an ASF is gone. Unless the person has developed another way to obtain that feeling, he may become depressed or begin acting out in other ways. Therefore, in Phase 1, the person's capacity to release FSs and remain emotionally stable should be assessed.

For example, if a person has been suicidal because of his destructive gambling behavior, then removing the FS driving the gambling behavior would give the person hope of a better life.

On the other hand, if the gambling has been used as a way to cope with a pre-existing depression that has become, at times, suicidal, then removing the FS would be contraindicated. In this case, clear the depression and other issues that the person has been unable to cope with except by using the addictive behavior.

2. History: The second purpose of Phase 1 is to obtain a general history of the person's addictive behavior— when it began, frequency over the years, periods of abstinence, attempts to quit, et cetera.

This phase also assesses whether there is likely to be a comorbid dynamic, such as anxiety or trauma symptoms, that may need to be addressed before treating the compulsive behavior.

If the person has a problem with depression or anxiety that preceded the addictive behavior, those issues may require treatment prior to focusing on the addictive behavior. The clinical experience of the therapist should determine the appropriate course of treatment.

3. Motivation: In Phase 1, another crucial evaluation is made—is the behavior the result of the motivation to either "avoid a feeling" or to a "seek a feeling"? The evaluation of the cause of the behavior determines the choice of treatment.

If the person is performing the behavior because he is avoiding a feeling, then the appropriate treatment is to process the memories, images, and feelings that the person is avoiding.

If the person is performing the behavior in order to experience a positive feeling, then FS treatment is indicated.

Because addictive behavior often does "double duty," alternating between the avoidance and seeking feeling dynamics, the focus of treatment may focus on one dynamic and then switch to the other dynamic.

ImTT Press, publisher

Phase 2: Phase 2 is the preparation phase. The Feeling-State Theory is explained, describing how behaviors can become fixated to desired feelings—the creation of the FS. The protocol of breaking that fixation using the IDP is described. In addition, the possibility that an underlying trauma may surface is explained, as well as the explanation of the use of ImTT to process the traumatic memory.

The P/TRP may be used on a simple emotional pain for the purpose of training the person in this approach.

Phase 3: Phase 3 gets specific about the addictive behavior. The purpose of Phase 3 is to identify and process the FS. The exact dynamics of the behavior, from beginning to end, are identified, as are the specific feelings associated with the behavior. After identifying the FS, the FS is then processed with the IDP. Between sets of deconstructing the image, only ask about the changes in the image such as if the image is fading, blurring, or falling apart.

Do not ask questions that prompt association unless the FS appears to be not processing or a person reports experiencing a reaction that may interfere with the FS processing, such as anxiety. If this occurs, the source of the reaction will need to be assessed and, if necessary, treated.

If the ASF is a feeling of euphoria, rush, or intense excitement, the client may be reluctant to re-experience a feeling that could lead to relapse. Emphasize in your instructions that the client is not to experience the feeling but only notice the feeling as if from a distance. Perform the IDP on the image. The IDP will reduce the intensity of the feeling. After reducing the image with the IDP, then eliminate the feeling using the Euphoric Sensation Release Protocol. Performing the ESRP after the IDP on the image will allow the client to connect with the reduced feeling so that the feeling can be completely released without the client resistance caused by his fears of relapse.

The CPP is done in this phase whenever the FS is a Sensation-FS or when there is not enough time to complete Phase 4 during the session. Targets to be selected are areas of a person's life that are likely to have been affected by the FS.

The purpose of Step 16, in which the client is assigned "homework," is to enable the therapist to evaluate the addictive/compulsive behavior for any changes in the behavior. The homework may consist of specific tasks that, in the past, may have activated the FS or may consist of only asking the client to be aware of any changes in the intensity of his urges or frequency of the behavior.

Phase 4: In Phase 4 the negative image and cognitions underlying the FS are identified. Either an image related to a lack of the desired feeling or an actual memory is processed with ImTT.

Important Note: Phase 3 and Phase 4 are *repeated* until all the FSs are processed.

Also important, any avoidance behavior, such as eating, used to avoid feelings of anxiety should also be addressed before moving on to Phase 5.

Phase 5: Phase 5 consists of processing the intense negative self-images that were created as a <u>consequence</u> of the addictive behavior. These images did not exist prior to the addictive behavior.

Phase 6: Phase 6 focuses on the images and memories arising from previous attempts at stopping the addictive behavior. These images often create feelings of anxiety about relapsing, even months after the person is no longer performing the addictive behavior. Processing the images of relapse will allow the person to accept his current, non-compulsive state of mind.

ImTT Press, publisher

The Feeling-State Addiction Protocol

The FSAP Flow Chart

The FSAP flow chart illustrates the different steps of the FSAP. The FSAP processes the addictive behavior in the reverse direction in which it was created. Starting with the addictive behavior, the FSAP 1) processes the FS, then 2) the intensified desire for the feeling, and then 3) the trauma or negative event that has created the intense desire for the feeling.

People have many different negative cognitions and traumas. Discerning which trauma is related to the addiction before processing the FS would be both extremely difficult and unnecessary. Processing the FS first allows the NC and the underlying trauma to easily surface to awareness. In fact, sometimes the trauma begins to emerge before the FS is even completely processed.

Processing in the reverse direction that the addictive behavior was created ensures that the desired feeling, the negative cognition, and the trauma are directly related to the addiction.

ImTT Press, publisher

FSAP Flow Chart

Identify the addictive behavior

Identify the intensified ASF driving the behavior

Process the FS

(Created by the intensified ASF)

Process the intense desire for the feeling

(Intensified by being blocked)

Identify the negative cognition (NC)

that blocks experiencing the desired feeling

Float back to the event creating the NC

Process the trauma

ImTT Press, publisher

The Feeling-State Addiction Protocol

The words in italics are a script of questions the therapist might ask the client.

Phase 1: History and Evaluation

1.   Obtain history, frequency, and context of the addictive behavior.

2.   Evaluate the person for having adequate coping skills to manage negative feelings if the person is no longer using substances to cope. If the person is too fragile for releasing the addictive behavior, process the pain, terror, and traumas until he is capable of coping without the addictive behavior.

Phase 2: Preparation

3.   Prepare the person for doing the standard EMDR protocol—explanation of EMDR, safe place, container, et cetera.

4.   Explain the FSAP including the Feeling-State Theory and how fixated memories cause behavioral and substance addictions.

5.   Explain how addictive behavior can also be used to avoid memories and feelings.

Phase 3: Processing the FS

6.   Identify the specific aspect of the addictive behavior that has the most intensity associated with it. If the addiction is to a stimulant drug, then the rush/euphoria memories are usually processed first. However, if some other memory is more intense—process that first. The starting memory may be the first time or the most recent—whichever is most potent.

7.   Identify the specific self-referential positive feeling (ASF) linked with the addictive behavior.

8.   If the ASF is a drug-induced Sensation-FS of rush or euphoria, release the feeling-sensation using the Euphoric Sensation Release Protocol (ESRP). Then continue to Step 9. If the ASF is not a drug-induced Sensation-FS, go to Step 9 without doing the ESRP.

9.   Measure the intensity of the link between the feeling and the behavior using the PFS (0 — 10) scale. The PFS always measures the intensity of this link. (E.g., *When you imagine yourself smoking with your buddies, how intensely do you feel that you belong?*)

10.   Locate and identify any physical sensations created by the positive feelings.

11.   Have the client combine 1) visualizing performing the addictive behavior, 2) intensely experiencing the positive feeling and, 3) feeling the physical sensations.

                                                                       ImTT Press, publisher

12. Perform BLS until the PFS level drops to 0 or 1.

13. Scan body for any sensation. Perform BLS until there is no sensation related to the FS.

14. Process the hyper-need for the desired feeling. Obtain a SUDS level of the feeling as a general feeling not connected with the behavior. (*Can you feel your general desire to belong? connect? feel important? et cetera?*)

15. Perform BLS until the SUDS = 0 or 1.

16. Reevaluate the FS. Perform BLS until PFS = 0 or 1. (*When you think of the original memory, on a 0-to-10 scale, how intense is it now?*)

17. Give homework to facilitate evaluation of the progress of therapy and to elicit any other feelings related to the addictive behavior.

18. In the next session, reevaluate the addictive behavior for the feeling-state identified in the last session. If that FS is still active, continue processing. If the FS has been eliminated, evaluate for other FSs or avoidance dynamics, as appropriate.

19. Steps 5 - 18 are performed again, as necessary.

Phase 4: Process the NC underlying the FS

20. Identify the NC that underlies the feeling. (*What's the negative belief you have about yourself that makes you feel you can't belong? can't connect? aren't important? et cetera?*)

21. Use the float-back method to identify an event related to that feeling. If no event is identified, target the NC. (*Can you remember an event that made you feel that way?*)

22. Process with the standard EMDR protocol.

23. Install a future template related to the PC of trauma processing.

Phase 5: Process the NC caused by the FS

24. Determine the negative belief that was created as a result of the addictive behavior and have the client choose a positive belief.

25. Use the EMDR standard protocol to process the negative beliefs and install the positive beliefs.

Phase 6: Process the Memories and Images that May Cause Anxiety about Relapsing

26. Identify the image or memories related to expectations or anxiety about relapsing.

27. Process the identified image or memories with the standard EMDR protocol.

25   ImTT Press, publisher

Discussion of the FSAP

The FSAP establishes all the elements that must be processed in order to eliminate compulsive behavior resulting from a feeling-state. Because the FSs have such destructive and negative influences on a person's life, eliminating the addiction makes working through other issues easier; so treatment should stay focused on processing the FS even when other issues arise.

When processing the FS with the FSAP, if the person begins to associate with traumatic memories and the person can be reasonably brought back to processing the FS, then the FSAP processing should be continued. However, if the traumatic memory is too overwhelming and must be immediately worked through, that is not a problem. Diverging from the protocol is common.

After working through the trauma, return to the point in the protocol where the divergence occurred and continue with the FSAP processing where you left off. As long as all the elements of the protocol are done, the addictive behavior will be eliminated. Diverging from the protocol is perfectly acceptable. The FS isn't going anywhere until it is processed.

Phase 1: Phase 1 has three purposes:

1. Safety: The first purpose is to establish the general safety of the client for removing FSs. Feeling-states are very powerful dynamics that can serve to emotionally stabilize a person. When an FS is eliminated, that source of a desired feeling is gone. If a person has no other way to obtain that feeling, he may become depressed or may act out in other ways. Therefore, in Phase 1, the person's capacity to release FSs and remain emotionally stable needs to be assessed.

For example, if a person has been suicidal because of his destructive gambling behavior, then removing the FS driving the gambling behavior would give the person hope of a better life. On the other hand, if the gambling had been used to cope with a pre-existing depression that had become, at times, suicidal, then removing the FS would be contraindicated. In this case, use other treatments to treat the depression and other issues that the person has not been able to cope with except by enacting the addictive behavior.

2. History: The second purpose of Phase 1 is to get a general history of the person's addictive behavior—when it began, frequency over the years, periods of abstinence, attempts to quit, et cetera. This phase also assesses whether there is likely to be a comorbid dynamic such as anxiety or trauma symptoms that may need to be addressed first. If the person has a problem with depression or anxiety that preceded the addictive behavior, those issues may need to be treated prior to focusing on the addictive behavior. The clinical experience of the therapist should guide the appropriate course of treatment.

3. Motivation: In Phase 1, another crucial evaluation is made. The question is whether the behavior is the result of the person "avoiding a feeling" or a "seeking a feeling." The evaluation of the cause of the behavior determines the choice of treatment. If the person is performing the behavior because he is avoiding a feeling, then the appropriate treatment is to process the memories, images, and feelings that the person is avoiding. If the person is performing the behavior in order to experience a positive feeling, then FS treatment is indicated. Because addictive behavior is often utilized for both avoiding feelings and seeking feelings, the focus of treatment may switch back and forth from one dynamic to the other dynamic.

Phase 2: Phase 2 is the preparation phase. The Feeling-State Theory is explained, describing how behaviors can become fixated with desired feelings—the creation of the FS.

The protocol of breaking that fixation with BLS is described. In addition, the possibility that an underlying trauma may surface is explained, as well as the use of EMDR to process the traumatic memory. The client should be prepared for processing the trauma using standard EMDR protocol techniques of the safe place and container, et cetera.

Phase 3: Phase 3 gets specific about the addictive behavior. In this phase, the exact dynamics of the behavior, from beginning to end, are identified, as are the feelings associated with the behavior. The purpose is to identify an FS. After identifying the FS, the FS is processed using BLS. Between BLS sets, ask the person whether the intensity of the FS is increasing, decreasing, or staying the same. This keeps the person focused on the FS so that it can be processed.

Do NOT ask, "What's happening for you now?"

Only ask questions that prompt association when the FS appears to be not processing or a person reports experiencing a reaction that may interfere with the FS processing, such as anxiety. If this occurs, the source of the reaction will need to be assessed and, if necessary, treated.

If the ASF is a feeling of euphoria, rush, or intense excitement, the client may be reluctant to re-experience a feeling that could lead to relapse. In this situation, use the Euphoric Sensation Release Protocol to reduce the intensity of the FS before processing with the BLS.

During the processing of the FS, the trauma linked with the FS may surface. Continue processing the FS, if possible. Then process the trauma in Phase 4.

If the trauma is too intense to continue processing the FS, then process the trauma and finish processing the FS after processing the trauma.

The purpose of Step 21, in which the client is assigned "homework," is to enable the therapist to evaluate the addictive/compulsive behavior for any changes in the behavior. The homework may consist of specific tasks that, in the past, may have activated the FS or may consist of only asking the client to be aware of any changes in the intensity of his urges or frequency of the behavior.

Phase 4: In Phase 4 the negative cognition underlying the FS is identified. A float-back is done to identify the event that created the NC. Then the event is processed using the standard EMDR protocol.

Important Note:

Phase 3 and Phase 4 are repeated until all the FSs are processed.

Also important, any avoidance behavior, such as eating, to avoid feelings of anxiety should also be addressed before moving on to Phase 5.

Phase 5: Phase 5 consists of processing the intense negative self-images and memories that were created as a consequence of the addictive behavior. These images did not exist prior to the addictive behavior.

Phase 6: Phase 6 focuses on the images and memories arising from previous attempts at stopping the addictive behavior. These memories often create feelings of anxiety about relapsing even months after no longer performing the addictive behavior. Processing the memories of relapse will allow the person to accept his current, non-compulsive state of mind.

Why Don't Feeling-States Become More Intense When Doing BLS?

A common question for EMDR therapists is: Why don't feeling-states become more intense when doing BLS? When performing the standard EMDR protocol, positive feelings are strengthened during the installation phase by utilizing BLS.

So if positive feelings are strengthened when installing positive feelings, why don't the positive feelings embedded in the FS—and thus the compulsive behavior—intensify?

The answer to this question lies in the Adaptive Information Processing (AIP) model used to explain how EMDR processes traumatic events. According to the AIP model, a traumatic memory is stored in a neurally isolated state—subsequent experiences do not alter the traumatic memory. The consequence is that the traumatic memories do not adapt with subsequent life experience. In a traumatic memory, the person sees himself and the event from the standpoint of the person he was at the time of the event.

A 30-year-old man who was physically abused when he was 8 years old will still be 8 years old in his traumatic memory, with all the old feelings of helplessness that occurred at that time. The neurally isolated memory does not change or adapt, even though the man is no longer helpless. The BLS of EMDR de-isolates the memory so that new information, the experiences the man has had growing up, allows the memory to incorporate the adult perspective instead of only that of the 8-year-old boy.

The AIP model also explains why FSs are not strengthened when doing BLS. As with traumatic memories, the FS is a neurally isolated memory that does not change with new experiences. The BLS allows the FS memory to associate with other, less positive memories so that the person is allowed a more realistic view of subsequent experiences. A gambler whose FS-embedded feeling was feeling like "a winner" will have a more realistic view of his life when the FS, the neurally isolated memory, becomes associated with his painful experiences of losing.

ImTT Press, publisher

Euphoric Sensation Release Protocol

The purpose of the Euphoric Sensation Release Protocol (ESRP) is to reduce the intensity of the ASF before processing the image with the IDP. The ESRP should be used when the client feels uncomfortable about reexperiencing the intensity of the ASF. The ESRP can be especially useful when doing the FSAP since the FSAP requires that the client experience the feeling more intensely than the FSIP requires. However, the ESRP is useful for both protocols.

The script uses the term "euphoric" to describe the feeling. However, if the client uses a different word such as "rush," substitute the client's terminology instead of "euphoric."

Script: *The purpose of the Euphoric Sensation Release Protocol is to reduce the intensity of rush or euphoric feelings that are often part of the memory of a drug. For many people who have used drugs, remembering the original memory can be scary because intense euphoric feelings can be activated. Anyone who has tried to control these feelings can get scared of letting themselves experience those feelings again because they are afraid of relapsing. What we are going to do is release those feelings without you having to experience them. I'm going to take you through an easy breathing/visualization protocol that will help you release those euphoric or rush feelings. Okay?*

Now I'm going to ask you to see, as if from a distance, that euphoric feeling you experienced when you used (name the drug). Do not let yourself experience the feeling. Just look at it as if from a distance. Does that make sense to you?

1. *When you think of using (name the drug), can you notice the euphoric feeling?*

2. *Where is that euphoric sensation located in your body?*

3. *What color is the euphoric sensation?*

4. *From now on, I don't want you to think of anything but the color. Forget everything else. Just focus on the color, okay?*

5. *Where is the* [state color] *located in your body?*

6. *Visualize the* [state color] *as being composed of tiny, tiny, little* [state color] *particles.*

7. *Take a slow breath and visualize breathing into the* [state color] *particles.*

8. *As you breathe out, see the tiny* [state color] *particles moving directly out of your body.*

9. *Breathe into the center of your brain and release the tiny* [state color] *particles out the center of your forehead.*

10. *Breathe into the center of your brain and release the tiny* [state color] *particles out your eyes.*

11. *Breathe into your chest and release the tiny* [state color] *particles down your arms and out the palms of your open hands.*

12. *See your spine as being composed of guitar strings that go from the bottom of your spine to the top of your head. Breathe into the guitar strings; and as you breathe out, release the tension on the guitar strings and see the tiny, tiny* [state color] *particles radiate out in all directions as you release the tension on the lower guitar strings.*

13. *See the tiny [state color] particles radiate out in all directions as you release the tension on the middle guitar strings.*

14. *See the tiny, [state color] particles radiate out in all directions as you release the tension on the upper guitar strings.*

15. *Breathe into your abdomen and release the tiny [state color] particles out your navel area.*

16. *Breathe into your abdomen and release the tiny [state color] particles down your legs and out the bottoms of your feet.*

17. *See a spot 6 inches below your feet, between your feet...breathe into that spot... and see the tiny [state color] particles drain down your body, go through the spot, and be absorbed into the earth...see the [state color] particles drain down your body, go through that spot, and be absorbed...absorbed...absorbed into the earth.*

18. *Place your feet flat against the floor. See a six-inch sphere 18 inches beneath your feet. Breathe into the sphere...breathe into the sphere and see the tiny [state color] particles release from the sphere...see the tiny, tiny [state color] particles releasing from the sphere.*

19. *Breathe into your heart...breathe into your heart and release the tiny, tiny [state color] particles out your heart...releasing the tiny [state color] particles out of your heart.*

20. *Breathe into the depths of your heart...breathe into the deep, deep depths of your heart and release the tiny, tiny [state color] particles from the depths of your heart... releasing the tiny [state color] particles from the deep depths of your heart.*

21. *Breathe into your throat...breathe into your throat and release the tiny [state color] particles out your throat...releasing the tiny [state color] particles out of your throat.*

22. *Breathe into your voice...breathe into the depths of your voice and release the tiny [state color] particles from your voice...releasing the tiny [state color] particles from the deep depths of your voice.*

23. *Breathe into the right side of your brain...breathe into the right side of your brain and release the tiny, tiny [state color] particles out the right side of your brain... releasing the tiny [state color] particles out the right side of your brain.*

24. *Breathe into the left side of your brain...breathe into the left side of your brain and release the tiny, tiny [state color] particles out the left side of your brain...releasing the tiny [state color] particles out the left side of your brain.*

25. *Breathe into the front of your brain...breathe into the front of your brain and release the tiny, tiny* [state color] *particles out the front of your brain...releasing the tiny* [state color] *particles out the front of your brain.*

26. *Breathe into the back of your brain...breathe into the back of your brain and release the tiny, tiny* [state color] *particles out the back of your brain...releasing the tiny* [state color] *particles out the back of your brain.*

27. *Breathe into the center of your brain...breathe into the center of your brain and see the tiny, tiny* [state color] *particles, releasing, radiating out in all directions from the center of your brain...see the tiny* [state color] *particles, releasing, radiating out in all directions from the center of your brain.*

28. *Breathe into your mind...breathe into the deep depths of your mind and release the tiny* [state color] *particles from your mind...releasing the tiny* [state color] *particles from the deep depths of your mind.*

29. *Breathe into the core of your self...breathe into what you think of as the core of your self...and release the tiny, tiny* [state color] *particles out the core of your self... releasing the tiny* [state color] *particles out the core of your self.*

30. *Imagine that you are about to yawn. Imagine that you are yawning a deep, wide yawn. As you yawn, see the* [state color] *particles release from the core of your self...as you feel the yawn throughout your whole body...as you feel the yawn throughout your whole body, see the tiny* [state color] *particles releasing from the core of your self.*

31. *Scan your body to see if there are any of the* [state color] *particles left in your body. If there are, breathe into that part of your body and then breathe the tiny* [state color] *particles out the pores of your skin in that area.*

32. *Now let's re-evaluate the euphoric sensation. Is the feeling less charged?*
    [The person should state that the intensity of the euphoric feeling has been reduced.
    For the FSAP: If the feeling is less intense, continue processing the FS with BLS.
    For the FSIP: Obtain a PFS level. If the PFS is greater than 1, do the IDP again targeting either the same image or another image related to the same drug.
    If the feeling has not been reduced, reevaluate the situation.]

                                                           ImTT Press, publisher

Chapter 3

Feeling-State Dynamics

Resisting "Letting Go" of the Addictive Behavior

No one wants to "let go" of an addictive behavior. No matter how disastrous the consequences have become, there is always a part of the person that wants to continue doing the behavior.

Addictions are difficult to "let go" of because an intensely desired survival feeling (the ASF) has become linked with the behavior. Asking a person to quit shopping who has an FS of "belonging" linked with "shopping in expensive stores" is really asking them to give up the intensely desired feeling of "belonging" that they want to experience. That is why addictions are so difficult to overcome. Not doing the behavior means that the person does not experience the feeling. As long as the behavior is identified with the desired feeling, the person will not want to stop doing the behavior.

Once the person is able to consciously differentiate between the desired feeling and the behavior, their resistance to breaking the linkage between the feeling and behavior is reduced. Identifying the specific ASF will allow the person to understand exactly what feeling he is seeking so that the person's own rational mind can realize how illogical it is to think that there is any necessity to do that particular behavior in order to obtain the desired feeling.

Alice's FS linking her desire to buy expensive clothes with the feeling of being "special" was created when she was 15 years old—Alice's mother bought her expensive clothes for the first time. This experience made Alice feel intensely special, which created the FS. After that shopping trip, whenever Alice needed to feel "special," Alice would buy expensive clothes. Once the feeling of being "special" was identified and Alice became aware that the FS was created when she was 15, Alice realized that her life was being "run" by her 15-year-old self. After that realization, Alice had no difficulty allowing the FS to be eliminated.

                       ImTT Press, publisher

Identifying the Feeling-State

Identifying both the behavior and the feeling in the FS is crucial and often not obvious. The following is an example of what happens when the feeling-state is not identified correctly:

Jim was a 35-year-old male with a history of problem gambling. The previous week he had lost $800 playing poker (Texas Hold'em). He identified what appeared to be his most intense positive memory playing poker occurred when he came back from having lost all but a few chips and won everything—winning against the odds with a poor beginning hand. After that, he believed that he could win against the odds and that "If I can win against the odds, then I can do anything."

Jim stated that the Positive Feeling Scale (PFS) equaled 7 (PFS =7). After several sets, the PFS was still 7.

Nothing had changed. We had worked on the positive feeling of "winning," but because it was not the feeling embedded in the FS, nothing happened, either good or bad.

During the history taking, Jim had described a time in his life when he would organize a poker night with his buddies 3-4 nights per week. After discussing this further, Jim identified the feeling of "camaraderie." Upon reflection, he recognized that playing poker with strangers activated the feeling of camaraderie that he experienced with his buddies. The "camaraderie" feeling had a PFS = 7. After two sets of processing, the PFS dropped to 0. He then realized that the people he played poker with the week before were not really his friends. At that point, he realized that he really did not fit in with those people and that they were just acquaintances who were out to take his money.

Identifying the <u>Real</u> Addictive Behavior

Identifying the specific behavior that is linked with the feeling may not be obvious. Any behavior is necessarily composed of many different sub-behaviors. Many of those sub-behaviors, however, are only important because they lead to the goal—the specific ASF that is embedded in the FS. These sub-behaviors are the pathway to the FS. Once the FS is processed, those sub-behaviors will stop having any importance. The person will no longer do them since they do not lead to a goal—the feeling embedded in the FS. Thus the first step towards identifying the FS is to identify which specific sub-behavior is linked with the intensely desired feeling.

Dustin had been struggling with sex addiction for over 10 years. When Dustin first described his sexual compulsion, he focused his description on the women he had sex with. He talked about the excitement of obtaining their cell phone numbers, making the connection, and other behaviors, including the sexual conquest. While all these behaviors were mildly exciting to him, his eyes just didn't "light up" enough to indicate that any of these behaviors were linked with the ASF.

The behavior that was intensely exciting for Dustin only became obvious when he described his behavior after the sexual experience—telling a friend about his latest conquest. All the previous behaviors were just the lead-up to the moment when he could tell a friend of his latest conquest. The telling to his friend about his latest conquest was the behavior that was fixated in the FS.

 ImTT Press, publisher

Identifying the Assured-Survival Feeling

The Feeling in the FS is <u>Always</u> Self-Referential

The feelings embedded in the FS are always self-referential—not other-referential. For example, Jane had a codependent relationship with her abusive boyfriend. At imes she reacted appropriately to his abusive behavior and left him . After a few days, Jane would then express a desire to go back to him because, as she stated it, "I love him."

Jane's feelings of "love" for her boyfriend were caused by her desire to feel "special" that was linked with him. Breaking the link between feeling "special" and her ex-boyfriend eliminated her urge to be with him that she had interpreted as "love."

Focusing treatment on Jane's "love" for her ex-boyfriend would have been focusing on the wrong dynamic—the other-referential feeling. In FS treatment, the feeling to be identified is always the feeling the person has about himself—the self-referential feeling.

The distinction is easier to notice when identifying FSs in regard to other types of compulsive behavior, such as a shopping compulsion.

Betty's Shopping Compulsion:

- Betty has a compulsive behavior to buy expensive clothes.

- Betty's feeling about the clothes is that they are "wonderful." (Other-referential)

- Betty's feeling about herself when buying clothes is "important." (Self-referential)

- Betty's feeling of "I am important" is the feeling embedded in the FS.

In every discussion about identifying FSs, the "feeling" the therapist is seeking to have the client identify is always a self-referential feeling.

The Feeling in the FS is <u>Always</u> Self-Referential

Methods of Identifying the ASF

As described previously, a feeling-state is composed of any desired ASF and any behavior. This means that there is no obvious connection between feelings and behaviors. However, identifying the exact behavior and feelings are key elements of the FS therapeutic process. This lack of any obvious or necessary connection between any specific feeling and any specific behavior is the most difficult aspect of FS treatment.

An example of the challenge of identifying the precise FS is Terri, who had a shopping compulsion. Terri was easily able to identify the feeling of excitement when she imagined herself shopping. However, Terri's excitement was really an excitement of anticipation—anticipation about, as she put it, "getting what I want." In other words, the feeling of "getting what I want" was the real feeling she was seeking, not the feeling of excitement.

Anytime a person performs an addictive behavior, the entire FS is present. This means that any addictive event can be processed resulting in the entire FS being broken. The problem is that, for most people, the addictive behavior has become almost automatic, meaning that there is little awareness of any feelings linked with the behavior.

For example, a smoker may only notice the feeling of relaxation. As will be explained later in the book, relaxation is not an ASF. The person will most likely be unaware of the feeling of "belonging," for example, linked with smoking. If the feeling of "relaxation" was processed, instead of "belonging," there would likely be no change in the person's behavior. Thus, identifying the correct ASF is crucial in order to eliminate the addictive/compulsive behavior.

The following methods are useful for identifying the ASF.

1. **Context:** The context in which the person performs the behavior can be useful in identifying the ASF.

Example: Jeb would go from one smoking location to another until he found someone to smoke with. He was seeking the feeling of "fitting in."

2. **The original memory:** Identifying the event in which the FS was created allows the entire context of the FS to be understood. This makes identifying the feeling easier and will include subtle aspects of the feeling that the person is not aware of. In addition, when a person realizes that he is being compelled by an event that occurred when he was 12 years old, for example, he will have little reluctance to letting the FS go.

Example: Rick identified that his smoking addiction began when he was 13 years old when some older boys invited him to smoke. Even though he coughed through his cigarette, an older boy told him "You done good." From that point, smoking was linked with "belonging." When Rick realized what the event was that created his smoking behavior, he had no resistance to eliminating the FS.

3. **Identifying the feeling the person has just before he begins the behavior. Ask:** "*What do you feel just before you do the behavior?*"

Example: A woman with a compulsion to eat a large pizza experienced the feeling that everyone in her family was taking a slice of pizza when she began to eat. The eating of pizza had become linked with the feeling of connection with her family.

4. Morphing the image:

ASFs can sometimes be identified by allowing the mind to "morph" or change the image of the behavior.

Script: *"What I want you to do now is to allow your mind to change the image into anything it wants to. Just let your mind change the image."*

Example: A woman had a memory of buying and eating candy as a child. When asked to allow her mind to morph the image, the image changed into a bird flying. This shift in image allowed her to identify the feeling of "freedom" that she had associated with the behavior of eating candy.

5. For codependence, Ask: *"What's the most positive experience you've ever had with him/her?"*

This question is useful when the person has difficulty releasing a relationship or continues an abusive one. The FS links the "loved" person with the intensely desired feeling.

For the codependent person, leaving the "loved" person means not obtaining the desired feeling.

As with all FSs, negative experiences don't change the fixation. That is the reason a person cannot be "talked out" of a codependent relationship. What makes the person resistant to leaving or changing the relationship is that the ASF is linked with the "love" person. Once the feeling is de-linked from the person, the FS will no longer override the negative experiences. Once the FS is eliminated, the person will be able to appropriately assess the relationship, taking into account both the positive and negative experiences with the loved" person.

Example: When Sarah was asked what the most positive experience was that she had had with her boyfriend, she replied, "We were lying on the couch, and he was holding me. I experienced a wonderful feeling of wholeness." Breaking the link between the "wholeness" feeling and her boyfriend ended Sarah's desire to continue the relationship with her abusive boyfriend.

6. Euphoria: Ask: *"When did you feel the most euphoric when doing this behavior?"* The "euphoric" question may help the person remember a positive event associated with the behavior. The feeling may not actually be a euphoric feeling, but the "euphoria" question will enable the person to identify the feeling that was really wanted.

Example: When Jack was asked what was his most euphoric time smoking, he remembered an event that occurred with his buddies from his football team when he was in junior high. The feeling was actually a feeling of "belonging." The question about feeling "euphoric" just helped him identify the event.

7. Fantasy: Fantasy can be used to identify ASFs. The person is asked to make up a scenario about what is happening when performing the behavior.

Script: *"I'd like you to make up a scenario about whatever is happening. Just fantasize whatever feels right when you're doing that behavior."*

Example: Sally fantasized that, when she was buying clothes, her mother would be looking at her with approval because the clothes enabled her to fit in with the "proper" people. Her mother's approval made her feel "special."

ImTT Press, publisher

More on Using Fantasy to Identify Feeling-States

A feeling-state is a fantasy. Even when the originating event is identified, the FS memory is still a fantasy. For example, FSs related to "I'm a winner when I play poker" and "When I smoke Marlboro cigarettes, I'm a man" are fantasies. This "fantasy" effect means that, even when the original event and feelings are identified, there may be other psychological elements embedded in the FS that were not part of the actual event.

For example, Art's "smoking" FS linked smoking with belonging. The original event involved smoking with an admired older boy. The feeling embedded was that he "fit in" with the "special" people.

When asked to create a fantasy based on that memory, Art fantasized that he was part of a group of "special" people. The feeling embedded was that he "fit in" with the "special" people. The fantasy allowed Art to have a more specific understanding of the general feeling of "belonging." The fantasy contained all the psychological elements of the FS that was causing the smoking addiction. The fact that the fantasy did not actually happen was not important. What *was important* was to process the fantasy "memory" that was creating the addictive/compulsive behavior.

What is psychologically real determines feeling and behavior.

What causes the compulsive behavior is not what actually happened but the fantasy of what happened. Focusing on identifying the fantasy image gives both the therapist and the patient a freedom to explore the psychological contents of the mind with fewer constraints. Instead of trying to determine what actually happened, the focus is on the images that the mind created.

In addition to elaborating the FS, fantasies can also be used to identify FSs that are more challenging to identify. For example, FSs related to compulsive eating behavior can be elusive. A fantasy approach to identifying the FS is to have the person visualize an imaginary scenario of the most intensely euphoric scene of eating. That imaginary scenario will provide clues to the FS, and a scene containing the linkage between the food and the identified feeling can then be processed.

Jan had a food compulsion focused on cookies. She liked other sweets, but cookies were the most difficult for her to resist. Jan remembered that her grandmother would give her cookies after school. When Jan fantasized about the event, she imagined that she was in her grandmother's arms, feeling safe. Even though that specific event did not actually occur, as far as she could remember, the FS linking the feeling of safety with cookies was easily identified when Jan allowed herself to fantasize about the event.

ImTT Press, publisher

Which Memory to Process?

A person with a compulsion will have acted out that behavior many times. The question is which memory to process. The first? most recent? the most intense?

Because the FS is activated every time the compulsive behavior is performed, theoretically, the FS can be processed utilizing any memory. However, the memory of the event in which the FS was created is usually the best memory to process. The memory of this event contains all the information and emotional resonance that created the FS. When the person can identify this event, the FS will likely process quickly. Identifying the originating event also helps the person understand why he has been suffering from the compulsion.

Understanding the original event may facilitate processing of the FS because the person can more easily separate in his mind the feeling from the behavior. Realizing that his life is being determined by an event that happened at 13 years old, for example, will often provide a person with a compelling motivation to process the FS.

Sometimes, the originating event cannot be identified. The person may not have any idea when the compulsion began. In this situation, choose the most intense event, which may or may not be the most recent.

Whether you process the memory of the originating event or a different event, enhancing the memory with additional fantasy elements will allow for a more complete processing of the FS.

Multiple Feeling-States

Compulsive/addictive behaviors can be the result of multiple feeling-states. Think of each FS as a "force vector" which, when added all together, creates the intensity of the craving for a particular behavior. The more FS force vectors and/or the larger each vector, the more intense the craving.

When multiple FSs are present, processing one FS removes one of the vectors that make up the cravings. When the client returns for the next session, the other FS vectors will still be there. However, if an FS is eliminated, there should be some change in the person's compulsive/addictive behavior—a change in frequency, intensity, or duration.

Gene's experience is an example of a change in the compulsive behavior that occurs even though other FSs are still present. In Gene's previous session, the FS of "belonging" linked with smoking had been eliminated.

When Gene was asked if there had been any change in his smoking behavior, he stated that he was still smoking 10 cigarettes—as many as before the session. When asked if he was smoking complete cigarettes, Gene looked startled and said, "No." He was unaware that he was smoking only half a cigarette at a time—that is 10 half-cigarettes. Gene's smoking behavior had actually been cut in half—5 cigarettes. He just hadn't noticed. So the elimination of the "belonging" FS changed Gene's behavior even though there were other FSs remaining that were activating his current smoking behavior.

Gene's experience also illustrates why a detailed understanding of the compulsive behavior is important. Changes in behavior can be easily overlooked. People more easily notice what **is** happening; people often don't notice what is **not** happening. The "not happening," however, is the goal of treatment. Becoming aware of signs of progress in treatment is useful for both therapist and client.

The following diagram illustrates the "multiple FSs" concept:

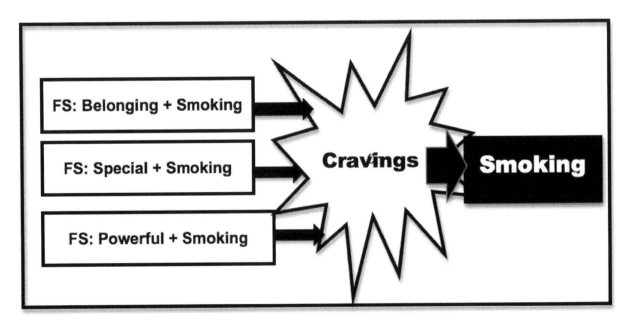

ImTT Press, publisher

Example of a Timeline for Creating Multiple FSs

Multiple FSs linked to the same behavior can be created over a period of time. The following diagram illustrates how one behavior, smoking, can be linked to multiple FSs. In the diagram, a boy experiences a trauma at 5 years old, creating the belief "no one wants me." At age 11, he experiences a positive event when he feels accepted by a group of boys for daring to smoke with them. An FS (FS1) is created linking smoking with the feeling of "acceptance."

During the boy's adolescence, he often feels awkward around girls. The feeling of awkwardness continues to bother him and often makes him shy around women. At age 18, a woman tells him how sexy he looks when he smokes, which makes him feel "manly." So smoking behavior is also linked with feeling "manly" (FS 2).

The result is that smoking is now linked with two separate and distinct FSs. Which FS is stronger will depend on the intensity of the desire for the ASF at the time the FS is created.

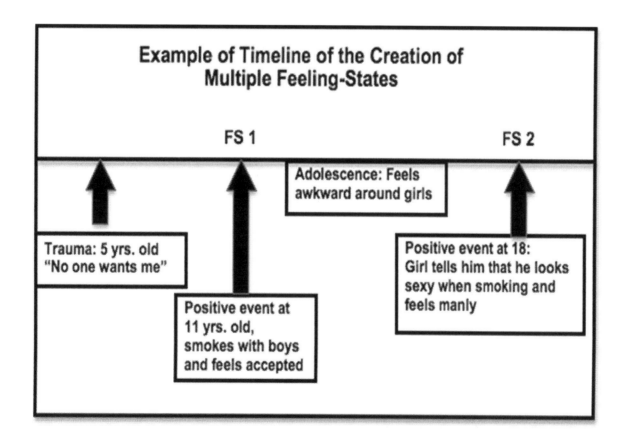

Example of Timeline of the Creation of Multiple Feeling-States

FS 1

FS 2

Adolescence: Feels awkward around girls

Trauma: 5 yrs. old "No one wants me"

Positive event at 18: Girl tells him that he looks sexy when smoking and feels manly

Positive event at 11 yrs. old, smokes with boys and feels accepted

                                       ImTT Press, publisher

Less Intense Feeling-States Emerge

After More Intense FSs are Released

Multiple FSs linked with a compulsive behavior are common. Attempting to identify all the FSs in the beginning is not useful, necessary, or even possible. The first FS identified is usually the most intense with the most effect on behavior. Once that FS is released, other, less powerful FSs will often emerge. The less powerful FSs are then processed as they emerge.

A useful metaphor for the emergence of addiction FSs is the Bright Light metaphor.

Bright Light Metaphor:

A strong, bright light will hide less intense lights like the sun hides the stars. In the same way, an intense FS will hide less intense FSs. The most intense FS is the most easily identified. Once the most intense FS is eliminated, other less intense FSs will surface. These FSs were always present but could not be discerned until the brightest one was eliminated. Because less intense FSs are hidden by more intense FSs, there is no clinical advantage to attempting to identify more than one FS at a time. Process each FS as it emerges.

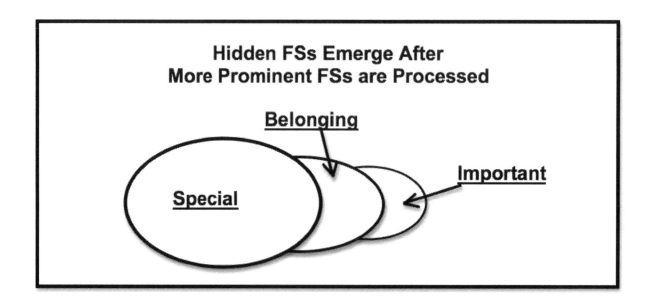

Substitute Addictions

Substitute addictions are behaviors that substitute for the addiction that is really wanted.   Johnston presented for therapy with a problem with alcohol. He began drinking seriously at age 22 when he realized that, if his blood tested positive for THC, he was not going to be able to get the job he wanted. Previously, he had been smoking marijuana every day. He began smoking marijuana when he was 17, in order to fit in with the "in" crowd. As he stated it, grass was his drug of choice, but if not that, then alcohol would do.

For Johnston, alcohol was not his primary addiction; his primary addiction was marijuana.   In addition to alcohol, he also appeared to have an "addictive personality," becoming easily obsessed with video games and other behaviors that he would do intensely for a time and then just "let go" of.

For Johnston, focusing treatment on any of these behaviors would have likely created a game of Whack-A-Mole—the compulsive behavior changing from one behavior to another behavior.   In other words, once one behavior would have been processed, another behavior would emerge.

To   avoid   playing   Whack-A-Mole with different addictive behaviors, the focus for treatment should be on the original addiction—in Johnston's case, marijuana.   There may be additional FSs associated with the other behaviors, but the original addictive behavior should be processed first. Then, when you process the FSs of the other behaviors, you can be sure that you are not just pushing the FS   of   the   original   addiction   onto another behavior.

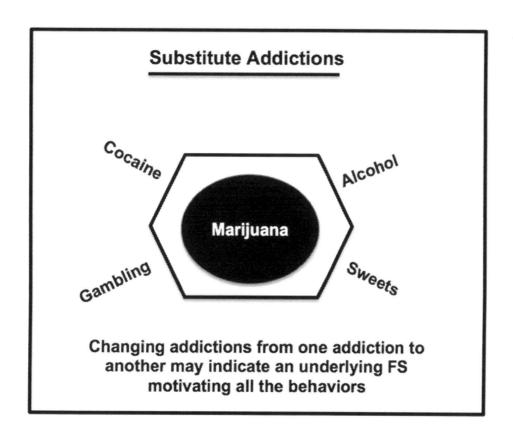

More On The Whack-A-Mole Question

A common occurrence of people with compulsions/addictions is that, when they stop doing one behavior, another behavior pops up. People who exhibit this dynamic are sometimes referred to as having an "addictive" personality. How is feeling-state work any different?

This question is partly discussed previously. When a person just stops doing a specific addictive behavior, another behavior is often substituted for the previous addictive behavior. A person who stops drinking, for example, may smoke or eat more. These are, as described above, substitute addictions.

Feeling-State processing is different from behavioral-management types of therapies. FSs create addictive behavior. If the cause of the addictive behavior is eliminated, then there is no reason for a substitute behavior—no FS motivating the person to find some other behavior in which to experience the ASF. That's why, when an FS-caused addictive behavior, such as gambling, is eliminated with FS treatment, no other behavior takes its place. In other words, with FS treatment, the Whack-A-Mole pattern is not created.

Removing the Cause

Not Managing the Symptom

Irrational and Distorted Thinking

An interesting effect of the FS treatment is that people realize how they have rationalized and distorted their thinking to justify their out-of-control behavior. Once the feeling-state is eliminated, their need for the rationalizing patterns is gone. Since the irrational thought patterns no longer serve a purpose, the rationalizations and distorted thought patterns begin to disappear.

For example, "chasing" behavior, in which a gambler thinks that the next bet will be a winner, usually resolves with little further therapy. People often describe this process as "waking up from a nightmare" or "having a demonic spell lifted." When they are no longer under the "spell" of the compulsion, their common sense reasserts itself.

These previously resistant-to-change cognitive distortions are easily discarded, usually without prompting, because they are no longer needed to justify the compulsive behavior.

The irrational and distorted cognitions used to justify compulsions disappear when the FS is released.

Reason: The cognitions no longer serve a purpose.

Feeling-States and Traumas are

<u>Different</u> Fixated Memories

Feeling-State Theory views trauma and neglect as events that create blockages that prevent the person from experiencing ASFs. The blockage that prevents a person from experiencing an ASF intensifies the person's desire for that ASF. Then the intensified ASF creates an FS when an event occurs that provides the needed feeling.

Traumas, on the other hand, create negative feelings from negative events. This means that the feeling fixated in the trauma (e.g., fear, pain, guilt, shame) and the feeling fixated in the FS (e.g., belonging, important) are totally different feelings, arising from completely different events. This means that memories arising from traumatic and neglect events require <u>separate processing</u> from the FSs created during a positive experience.

Even though the person is blocked by a traumatic event from experiencing the ASF, the normal desire for the ASF existed prior to the trauma; the trauma only blocked access to the ASF, intensifying the desire for the ASF. Thus, even though FSs may be related to trauma and neglect, FSs are *not* psychological defenses to avoid the associated negative feelings resulting from trauma and neglect

The flow chart describing the creation of a feeling-state (pg. 5) illustrates the connection between a trauma or an emotional deficit and the FS. Without the original trauma or neglect creating an intense desire for a feeling, the person would not have experienced the positive event with enough intensity to form an FS. Though the FS requires an intense desire for a feeling in order for the FS to be created, once the FS is created, the FS functions separately from the deficit that created the intensity of the desire.

Because the FS is its own separate memory, the FS must be treated separately.

Processing the trauma does not process the FS;

Processing the FS does not process the trauma.

Carol presented for therapy because she was crying every night since breaking up with her boyfriend. When Carol was asked the codependent question, "What's the most positive experience you ever had with your ex-boyfriend?" Carol replied that the most positive experience was the first time he took her dancing.

The feeling she experienced when dancing with her boyfriend was the feeling of being "special." Because of that event, the feeling of being "special" became linked with the boyfriend—and an FS was created. The "special" FS was eliminated in Phase 3 with FS treatment. Then the underlying trauma was targeted.

The trauma that began the intensification of her desire to feel "special" occurred when she was 5 years old. On her birthday, her father told her that she wasn't anything special and that no one would ever really want her. That trauma was processed after the FS ("special" + boyfriend) was eliminated.

In the second session, Carol reported that she had stopped crying every night but that she still missed her ex-boyfriend a lot. Again, the question was asked, "What was the second most positive experience you ever had with your boyfriend?"

46   ImTT Press, publisher

This time she talked about another event that had occurred several months after the first event in which she also felt "special" with her boyfriend. As with the first event of dancing, another FS was created.

In other words, two different events created two FSs with the feeling of being "special" as the feeling embedded in the FS.

Carol's second FS was then eliminated. When identifying the underlying trauma, Carol said that it was the same trauma that had been processed the previous session. When thinking about that event, Carol stated that she no longer had any reactions to that memory. In other words, Carol's second FS still existed, even though the underlying trauma had been eliminated. When Carol returned for her next session, she reported that she no longer missed her ex-boyfriend and was moving on.

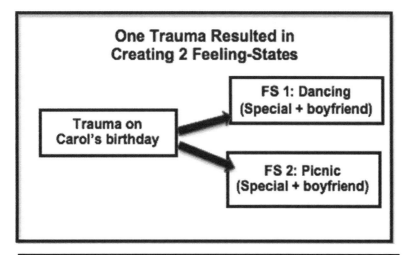

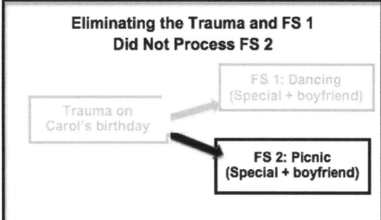

Carol's experience illustrates several important points:

1. **One trauma blocking ASFs can result in the formation of multiple FSs.**
2. **Different FSs can have the same embedded feeling.**
3. **Processing the trauma does not process the FS.**
4. **Each fixated memory, negative or positive, requires separate processing.**

ImTT Press, publisher

What is not an Assured Survival Feeling

Not all feelings that people report as being associated with an addictive behavior are the feelings that are actually embedded in the FS.

Feelings that are *not* ASFs

When people are asked what feeling they experience when performing a compulsive behavior, they will often answer with words such as "comfort," "relaxation," "soothing," "peacefulness," or "calm." The problem is that these feelings are not the feelings fixated in the FS. If these feelings are targeted, the behavior will not change.

Smoking may indeed calm a person down, but comfort is not the feeling embedded in the FS. Rather, comfort is the result of getting the desired ASF. So if the feeling of "belonging" is linked with smoking, a person who is feeling anxious because he feels lonely will feel "comfort" as a result of experiencing the feeling of "belonging" activated by smoking.

Calm, comfort, relaxation, peacefulness, soothing, and other quiet types of feelings are not the types of feelings embedded in FSs. These feelings are the *result* of getting powerful ASFs met. There is not a drive to feel calm. A person wants to feel calm only when they are upset. Remove the reason for the upset, and the desire to feel calm goes away.

Contrast the feeling of calm with the feeling of "being alive." The desire to feel "alive" is a powerful motivating force that drives behavior. Unlike the feeling of "being alive," the desire to feel calm only exists as a result of a person's feeling of being agitated in some way. The desire to feel "alive" is ever present and is often a driving force behind addictive behavior.

A person identifying the urge to feel calm or peaceful may be pointing to another psychological dynamic—avoidance. As previously noted, an addictive behavior can do double-duty. On the one hand, the behavior may be part of an FS with the person compelled toward doing the behavior in order to experience a desired feeling. On the other hand, the behavior may also be a way of avoiding other feelings such as anxiety. If a person is using addictive behavior for both purposes, both dynamics will need to be processed.

What's *NOT* an Assured-Survival Feeling

Calm   Peaceful   Comfort   Relaxation   Soothing

Urges and Cravings

Focusing treatment for compulsions/addictions on the urges or cravings a person experiences could be compared to a therapist's responding to a person who needs oxygen by focusing on the <u>urge</u> for oxygen rather than the oxygen. What the person needs is oxygen, not the urge.

In the same way, targeting the <u>urge</u> to gamble or to smoke marijuana is missing the point. The focus for treatment should be on the feeling that the person desires. For a person suffering from a compulsion or addiction, the desired feeling is the "oxygen" he needs, not the urge.

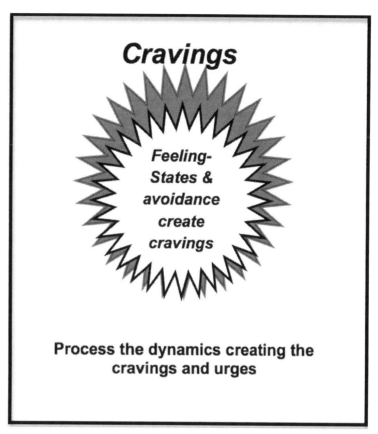

Cravings

Feeling-States & avoidance create cravings

Process the dynamics creating the cravings and urges

Dustin felt the urge to have sex and tell a friend, but he was not aware of his desire to feel like "Big Man on Campus"—Dustin's oxygen. Sarah felt the urge to be with her ex-boyfriend but was not aware of her desire to feel "wholeness"—Sarah's oxygen. Terri felt the urge to buy clothes but was not aware of her desire to feel "powerful"—Terri's oxygen. Dustin, Sarah, and Terri all experienced urges toward doing different behaviors. But what Dustin, Sarah, and Terri really wanted was the feeling each had linked with their behaviors.

Urges and cravings are only indicators that an FS may exist and needs to be processed in order to eliminate the addictive behavior.

That is why urges and cravings are not the focus of treatment. In FST, the focus for treatment is on the desired feeling, the oxygen, not on the urge for the desired feeling, the urge for oxygen.

The other dynamic that can create urges and cravings is avoidance—avoidance of negative feelings or memories. Just as with FSs, the focus for treatment should be on the dynamic that is the cause of the avoidant behavior. For example, if a person is drinking alcohol because their memory of witnessing someone die is too painful when they are sober, the target for treatment should be the painful memory. Once the memory is processed, the person will stop drinking because the person will not need to avoid the painful memory since the memory is no longer painful.

In summary, urges and cravings, whether the result of an FS or an avoidance dynamic, should not be the target for treatment. Rather, the dynamic creating the urges and cravings—either the FS or the avoidant dynamic—should be the focus for treatment.

ImTT Press, publisher

Safety

Cautions and Contraindications

Feeling-states are very powerful dynamics that can serve to emotionally stabilize a person. If a person has no social skills and has tremendous difficulties connecting with people, an FS of smoking linked with the feeling of "belonging" may help to maintain emotional stability. Whenever he feels lonely, he can smoke. Smoking takes much less effort to get the desired feeling of "belonging" than does interacting with people he doesn't know how to get along with.

When an FS is eliminated, that source of a desired feeling is gone. If a person has no other way to obtain that feeling, he may become depressed or start acting out in other ways. In Phase 1, the person's capacity to undergo changes to his psychological system needs to be assessed.

For example, if a person has been suicidal because of his destructive gambling behavior, then removing the FS driving the gambling behavior would give the person hope of a better life. On the other hand, if the gambling was more a way to cope with a pre-existing depression that had become, at times, suicidal, then removing the FS would be contraindicated. In this case, first treat the depression and other issues that he has been unable to cope with except by enacting the addictive behavior.

The fundamental concern is how the person will cope with the elimination of the addictive behavior. As often as the addiction has created chaos in a person's life, the addiction also may have been a source of emotional stability for coping with other psychological problems.

Cautions and Contraindications

Areas of Concern

1. **Feeling-states may stabilize an unstable personality.**
2. **Feeling-states may be utilized to minimize depression and anxiety.**

Solution—Before processing the FS:

1. **Stabilize the personality.**
2. **Process the psychological dynamics causing the depression and anxiety.**

ImTT Press, publisher

Chapter 4

A Discussion of Feeling-States

The precise identification of the FS is the most challenging and crucial element of the FS treatment process. Some feelings are easy to identify as being part of an FS, such as the feeling of "belonging". Feelings like excitement, however, may or may not be an FS. In addition, there are psychological dynamics like intergenerational joining and "being good" that require a more subtle discernment. This chapter discusses these various issues.

As described earlier, any ASF can become embedded in an FS. The only requirement is that the person has an intense desire for the ASF and that an intense positive experience occurs in which he experiences that ASF. The ASF then becomes fixated with the behavior.

A list of common FSs is provided in the Appendix.

There are the following two categories of feeling-states:

1. **Sensation-FS:** FSs created by the person's physiological reaction to a physical situation. The reaction could be the result of the body's reaction to a drug like heroin or to a dangerous situation like combat. Sensation-FSs include feelings such as euphoria and adrenalized excitement.

2. **Intensified-ASF-created FS:** Intensified ASF-created FSs have underlying experiences that block a person from experiencing an ASF. ASFs include feelings of safety, belonging, powerful, special, and connection.

Types of Feeling-States

1. <u>**Sensation-FS:**</u> **Created by reaction to the current situation (e.g. drugs or danger). No underlying trauma or deficit is necessary.**

2. <u>**Intensified-ASF-created FS:**</u> **Has underlying trauma or neglect that intensified the person's desire for the ASF.**

ImTT Press, publisher

The Sensation-FS

The Sensation-FS is created in reaction to two types of experiences—drugs or intense excitement-producing events. Composed entirely of the memory of the physiological reaction to an experience, the Sensation-FS is created as a result of the intensity of the euphoric or the "high" feeling. In the language of addicts, the Sensation-FS is often referred to as the "dragon" that is being "chased." This means that the Sensation-FS is an important FS to process because the Sensation-FS is a likely cause of relapse.

The good news is that the Sensation-FS is often the easiest to eliminate because the memory is easiest to recall, identify, and process. In addition, one of the differences between the Sensation-FS and a psychologically induced FS is that the Sensation-FS is not the result of an intensified psychological desire for a feeling such as "belonging." So Phase 4 of the FS treatment is not necessary.

Sensation-FSs created by:

1. Euphoric or "high" reaction caused by drugs.
2. Adrenaline "high"/excitement (intense feeling of being alive) triggered by reaction to danger.
3. Excitement that has become linked with a behavior such as eating.
4. Euphoric/Reward-FS reaction to approval.

ImTT Press, publisher

Drug-induced Sensation-FS

A Sensation-FS commonly occurs in response to drugs such as cocaine, heroin, and methamphetamine. While some people can take drugs and not create a Sensation-FS, other people just appear to be more physically/psychologically vulnerable to certain drugs. One person might be more reactive to cocaine, and another person, more reactive to heroin. The level of intensity of their reactions to the drug they are taking determines when a Sensation-FS is created.

As described above, the Sensation-FS is the easiest to identify and process. Because of its intensity, the Sensation-FS is also the FS that will cause a relapse. Therefore, the Sensation-FS should normally be processed first.

Alan is a good example of treatment for a Sensation-FS. Alan had been addicted to heroin for six years. He had entered rehab and had been sober for one year. At the beginning of a session, Alan stated that he had awakened that morning craving heroin again—something that had not happened for 10 months. He stated that he was likely to use again after the session.

Alan was asked to focus his attention on the memory of the sensation of the euphoria when shooting the heroin in his arm. He stated that his PFS was a 10. After three sets of processing, the PFS dropped to zero. The affect on his face went from a kind of "crazed" excitement to disgust at the thought of using heroin again after all the problems heroin had created in his life. Five years later, Alan continued to report that his craving for heroin had never returned.

Because Alan had come into the session with intense cravings, having him "tune into" the Sensation-FS was easy—he was already tuned into the feeling. When doing this step of the protocol for the first time, therapists and clients alike may approach with trepidation, fearing that the client will leave the session and relapse.

The client may have been successfully controlling his behavior and wanting to avoid any memory that would threaten his sobriety. But in order to process the FS, the client must be willing to access the memory of the euphoric feeling over which he has had to exercise such tight control in order to manage his behavior.

The good news is that the intensity of re-experiencing of the drug-induced FS can be reduced by either:

1. Using the FSIP because the Image De-Construction Protocol requries less "tuning into" than the FSAP. When using the FSIP, the client is instructed to "view" the feeling as if from a distance.

2. When using the FSAP, reducing the intensity of the FS by using the Euphoric Sensation Release Protocol before processing the FS with the FSAP.

After processing a Sensation-FS, therapists often describe how amazed they feel when watching the intensely excited affect fade from a client's face after only a few processing sets. Although therapists may hesitate when contemplating processing a drug-induced FS for the first time, using FS treatment to process non-sensation-FSs of behavioral addictions will build confidence in using the FS protocols for drug-induced FSs.

ImTT Press, publisher

Event-induced Sensation-FSs

There are two types of events that can induce a Sensation-FS. The first type of event involves the experience of danger. The second type of event that can create a Sensation-FS is when the person experiences intense excitement during an event. FSs arising from these events are discussed in this section.

Excitement: When is excitement an ASF?

1. **Danger-excitement is an AFS.**
2. **Excitement that occurs during an event may be intense enough to create an FS.**

ImTT Press, publisher

Excitement:
Sometimes it's the ASF in the FS
Sometimes it's not

When excitement IS the ASF:

Excitement in the form of an adrenaline rush can produce a Sensation-FS. The Adrenaline-Sensation-FS is created in situations involving danger. Activities such as combat, mountain climbing, firefighting, shoplifting, performing, and race car driving create the Adrenaline-Sensation-FS. Because the adrenaline surge is incredibly addictive, people will subsequently seek out danger, wanting to go back into combat, and risking injury and death to feel that "alive" feeling again. Excitement in this form—i.e., when it is fixated with dangerous behavior—is a Sensation-FS that should be processed before any other FSs are processed.

Any client who is an "Adrenaline junkie" should be evaluated for an Adrenaline-Sensation-FS.

Excitement can also be an ASF when the event is exciting for other reasons.

For example,

Betty's chocolate compulsion originated during her birthday party when she was 5 years old. The excitement of the party became linked with chocolate.

When excitement is NOT an ASF:

Excitement is not the ASF embedded in the FS when it is anticipatory excitement. When people are asked what they feel just before doing the addictive behavior, they commonly answer, "excited." They are usually referring to a feeling of excited anticipation.

Question: "What do you feel when you are about to go shopping?"

Answer: "I feel excited."

The problem for the therapist is that this type of excitement is unlikely to be an ASF, and processing the feeling "excitement" will not process the FS.

What the person is feeling is the excitement of anticipating getting what he wants. For example, if the person's FS is the feeling of importance linked with the behavior of buying expensive clothes, the desired feeling is the feeling of importance, not the feeling of excitement. The excitement the person is experiencing is anticipatory excitement, the anticipatory excitement of getting what the person really wants, which is the feeling of being important.

Summary: So excitement may or may not be an ASF depending on how the FS was created. If the FS was created in the context of participating in dangerous or intensely challenging events, the feeling of excitement is likely the embedded desired feeling. Excitement may also be an ASF if the excitement was generated during the event. On the other hand, if the feeling of excitement is activated by the anticipation of feeling the desired feeling, it is not an ASF.

Additional Dynamics

Creating Intensified-ASF-induced FSs

Chapter 3 discussed the creation of intensified ASF-induced FSs linked with feelings such as "belonging" and "special." This section describes additional psychological dynamics that can create FSs.

The Problem of Rewards — Killing the Spirit

In the book *Punished by Rewards*, Kohn (1999) recounts a research study with sixth graders. The children were given art supplies and then divided into two groups. One group could enjoy producing as much art as they wanted with the art supplies, but they were not paid for their art. The other group was paid for each piece of art produced.

After a period of time, they told the group that had been paid for their artwork that they could keep the art supplies but that they would not be paid for their art.
The group that had been paid for each piece of art produced more art while they were being paid. However, once the payments stopped, this group produced much less art than the other group that had never been paid. So by rewarding the children for producing art, the researchers were able to reduce the intrinsic reward of creating art.

In other words,

Rewards Kill Intrinsic Motivation.

The intrinsic reward system exists to reinforce behaviors that are, in themselves, functional in our lives. When we provide an external reward to reinforce a behavior, we are reducing the intrinsic feeling of reward that would be created by the behavior itself. The result is that we lose our feeling of connectedness to the behavior and lose our sense of integrity (being integrated) within ourselves. The further result is to need more external reinforcement for our various behaviors.

One of the problems with the external reward system is that a person can be rewarded for behavior that they don't enjoy doing or that is destructive.

The so-called "golden handcuffs" that some lawyers talk about, which bind them to practicing a particular area of law they no longer enjoy but can't quit because it is so highly lucrative, is an example of this.
As children we become hooked on the need for external rewards. Then as adults, we will look for ways to provide our own external rewards. These external rewards that we determine for ourselves may or may not support behavior that provides an internal sense of satisfaction.

An additional problem that "reward behavior" creates is that it displaces behavior that may actually be more functional. For example, suppose that, while you enjoy your work, you also have a pattern of rewarding yourself by watching TV. You may not even really enjoy the program you are watching, but you watch because you are getting your "reward." Instead of doing something that may be more intrinsically rewarding, you do a behavior that has been defined as a reward.

ImTT Press, publisher

THE FEELING-STATE THEORY & PROTOCOLS

Chapter 4 A Discussion of Feeling-States

We have a powerful desire to feel rewarded. That feeling of reward should come from the behaviors themselves; in other words, the behaviors should be intrinsically rewarding. Connecting an external behavior— e.g., eating chocolate—reduces the intrinsic reward of the original behavior and links chocolate to a powerful primal need. The result of linking chocolate with the powerful "reward" ASF is that chocolate will be eaten in order to experience the intensely desired "reward" feeling rather than because the person is responding to an intrinsic desire for chocolate as a food.

Approval and Reward

A reward is given to signal approval of behavior. The approval activates an intense positive sensation that can fixate our behavior toward other people's approval. This means that our behavior is shaped by the values and behaviors of others.

Even when we have control of what our own rewards will be, the values that are manifested in the rewards are often the result of what we have learned from others.

The result of rewards is that we are disconnected from our own internal dynamics. Like the children who stopped producing art once they were no longer rewarded, we stop paying attention to what actually gives us pleasure when our behavior is linked to being approved of and rewarded by others.

The solution is that NO behavior should be rewarded. Rather, each person should be paying attention to his own sense of internal pleasure. Instead of rewarding yourself with chocolate for working hard, eat chocolate because you want to eat chocolate and it fits into your priorities. If you lose weight and need new clothes, don't reward yourself by buying new clothes; buy new clothes because you need them and it fits your priorities.

Sensation (euphoric sensation) + Approved Behavior = Reward-FS

Processing the Reward Feeling-State

The Reward-FS is a Sensation-FS that connects the behavior necessary for the reward (the approv   ed-of behavior) with the intense reward sensation. Unlike the Sensation-FS that is produced by drugs, the Reward-FS links with behavior. The Reward-FS can be processed by having the client imagine a fantasy of being approved of by people important to the client and the euphoric sensation of being rewarded.

The Trap of Being Good

"Being good" means that you are congruent with an image of yourself that is usually a reflection of other people's values—e.g., parents, teachers, peers, et cetera—that you have acquired, often unconsciously, during childhood.

If "being good" means overworking, controlling your wife, or being altruistic, you'll reinforce these behaviors through your system of rewards, however you have constructed them.

In contrast with doing a behavior in response to an image, if you are doing a behavior because you want to do the behavior, there is no "being good" about it. You're just doing what you want to do. You are not fulfilling an image of yourself by doing the behavior. Instead, you are accomplishing what you want to accomplish. When you are "being good," you may or may not actually want to do the behavior that results in fulfilling the image of "being good." However, you may feel compelled to do the behavior in order to be a "good boy" or "good girl." The FS is the image of being a "good boy/good girl" and the ASF linked with the feeling.

Copyright 2016 by Robert Miller, PhD

Intergenerational Joining

> ## Intergenerational Joining
>
> An FS in which the person unconsciously mimics a behavior or quality of another person, often a parent. The person feels connected with the other person by having a characteristic of that person he wants to feel connected with.

Children have an intense need to have a relationship with their parents. A child may take on a specific behavioral pattern of a parent without ever realizing what he is doing.

For example, a divorcing father brought in his son for therapy to help his son handle the new family dynamics created by the father's divorce. The father came into the room and sat on the couch a certain way, talked a certain way, and used his hands a certain way. Afterwards, the son came into the room and sat on the couch the exact same way as the father, talked the same way as the father, and used his hands the same way as the father had used his hands. The son was clearly unknowingly patterning his behavior after his father.

This writer also had a similar experience. My father had a stroke and began having problems with word-find. He would start a sentence, not know what word to use, and then put some word, any word, into the sentence. I stayed with him for three weeks after he returned home from the hospital, and then I returned to work.

About six weeks later, I began having problems with word-find. At first I wondered if I had had a stroke. But upon reflection, I recalled a vivid memory, at the age of 10, watching my father's preparations for a speech he was giving at Toastmasters.

I was raised in a small Texas town, and people have often remarked on how my lack of Texan drawl belies my roots. Remembering that memory of my father made me realize that the reason I don't talk like a Texan is because I unconsciously learned how to talk like my father, who grew up on the East Coast.

Much to my surprise, the joining behavior of speaking like my father was dynamic, not just something learned in the past. Talking like my father was my way of connecting with my father and, heightened by my concern for him at the time of his stroke, my joining with him was strong enough that, when he had difficulty finding correct words, I began to have that same difficulty too. That is a measure of how powerful the desire to have a connection with a parent can be but also how powerful the FS is that it creates.

It happens occasionally that, when people recognize their behavior as being similar to their parent's, they are not entirely pleased. Their response is often "I'm not like him/her!"

Intergenerational joining does not contradict that. A person can be completely different from his parent and still have chosen, as a child, to feel bonded with his parent by unconsciously picking out some behavior of the parent's, meaningful to the child, and mimicking the behavior in order to feel connected to the parent. When the person does the behavior, he feels connected to his parent.

ImTT Press, publisher

While this discussion has focused on the need for connection with parents, behavioral mimicking, in order to feel bonded, can also be done with grandparents or any other person who the person feels a strong desire to have a relationship with. This is how behavior can be transmitted from one generation to another even when skipping a generation.

Intergenerational Joining-FSs can result in problems with alcohol, anxiety, anger, depression, or any behavior that a child unconsciously has chosen to mimic.

When intergenerational joining occurs, the FS consists of the mimicking behavior linked with the feeling of connection or bonding with the desired person. Eliminating the Joining-FS will allow the person to change his behavior and find his own way of acting in the world.

Example of joining-caused depression: How the thoughts causing depression and anxiety can be linked to a positive feeling

An FS can cause depression and anxiety. Imagine that a child is being yelled at by his father and being called "stupid." Even though this appears to be obviously painful, the child may form an image of the father approving of the child whenever the child calls himself "stupid."

So whenever the now adult "child" calls himself stupid, he feels connected with his fatherThe consequence is that calling himself "stupid" also makes the person feel depressed.

Example of Joining-Caused Depression

Father calls son "stupid."

Son forms image of father calling him stupid.

When son calls himself "stupid," he feels as if he is connected with his father.

Whenever son wants to feel connected with his father, he calls himself "stupid."

Son feels depressed and that he can't do anything right because he is "stupid."

ImTT Press, publisher

ImTT Press, publisher

Chapter 5

Different Addictions
Different Issues

Sex Addiction

While I am using the term "sex addiction" for ease of reference, there is really no such thing as a "sex" addiction—and what I mean by that is that "sex addiction" is *not* about the sex. As described previously, a behavior becomes compulsive only when an ASF has become linked with a behavior.

What the person is really seeking is the feeling linked with the sexual behavior. Once the feeling is de-linked from the behavior, whatever the behavior consists of is no longer of interest.

Sex Addiction:

It's NOT about the sex!

ImTT Press, publisher

Jake's Desire for "First Time" Sex

Jake presented for therapy because he had been caught soliciting a prostitute. He had been married for 10 years and had a moderately active sex life with his wife. However, whenever she would leave town, Jake would begin watching pornography and then find someone to have sex with.

Jake identified the experience he wanted as the feeling of being "accepted." When he had sex with a woman for the first time, Jake felt accepted. Once he had sex with a woman, she could no longer be the object of his compulsion. He could not obtain the feeling of "acceptance" with a woman he had previously had sex with.

Jake was able to trace his compulsion to an event that occurred during his college years when a woman he had desired for a long time finally had sex with him. Because of the circumstances of his childhood and the length of time that he had wanted to have a sexual relationship with the woman, Jake's feeling of being accepted was so intense that the feeling of being "accepted" became fixated with the behavior of having sex with a woman for the first time. Who he had sex with did not matter; what was important to him was that he had not had sex with her previously. Clearly, this was a compulsion that could not have been acted out within his marriage.

While it is true that Jake was caught while soliciting a prostitute, the fact that the woman was a prostitute was not of importance to Jake. What was important was that she be a woman with whom he had never had sex before. He had begun having sex with prostitutes several years prior to his arrest because having sex with prostitutes was easier; the entire process was faster because, unlike women who were not prostitutes, he didn't have to persuade a prostitute to have sex with him. So the "prostitute" aspect of his behavior was part of the mechanics of efficiency and was not relevant to the FS dynamics.

Once the FS was broken, all the activities Jake did leading up to that event were no longer of interest to him. For Jake, after processing the FS linking the feeling of acceptance with having sex with a woman for the first time, Jake found that his ritual behavior of viewing pornography leading to his sexually acting out was no longer interesting to him. His ritual of looking at pornography was only important because that behavior had become part of his pathway toward the compulsive behavior. Once Jake's looking at pornography   no longer led to what he wanted, he stopped looking at it.

Dan's "Massage Parlor" Compulsion

The focus of Dan's "sex" addiction was massage parlors. Dan had originally begun visiting massage parlors because he was trying to connect more with his own body. His mother had been physically withdrawn and emotionally unaffectionate when Dan was a child. As an adult, Dan sought out massages as a way of becoming more attuned to his own body.

During a massage, the masseuse touched his chest in a certain, non-sexual way. Though the touch was non-sexual, Dan experienced an intense feeling of connection with the masseuse— a feeling of bonding and connectedness that he had never experienced in his life. The massages quickly became sexual, and he sought this experience again and again—with that masseuse and with other masseuses.

ImTT Press, publisher

When I first began working with people with sex addiction, one of the aspects that seemed mysterious to me was that, in more than one case, the client would state that he was seeking "intimacy" at a massage parlor. The facts that he may not have been able to even talk with the masseuse because she spoke a different language and that he had to pay for the sex and that he might never see the woman again—those problems that would appear to any outside observer to be obstacles to intimacy did not interfere with Dan's experiencing a feeling of "intimacy" during the encounter.

The solution to the mystery of how one could obtain the feeling of intimacy in what is, for most people, a non-intimate situation requires an examination of what Dan meant when he identified "intimacy" as the feeling that he was seeking.

Dan was seeking a mother-child type of intimacy, not an adult-man-to-adult-woman type of intimacy. Having a masseuse that he could not converse with was one of the necessary elements for Dan to be able to act out the fantasy of the mother-child bonding. Conversation would have interfered with the fantasy he was creating. Dan's feeling-state was composed of the feeling of a "mother-child intimacy" bonding that had become fixated with sex at a massage parlor.

What is important to note is that what Dan really wanted was the feeling of the "mother-child intimacy," not the sex. The sex was the behavior through which he experienced the feeling of "mother-child intimacy," The mysterious case of "Intimacy at the Massage Parlor" was solved.

Victor's Sexual Addiction

Victor was a married 52-year-old engineer who began having problems with his sexual behavior when he was in his 30s. He had been attending Sex Addicts Anonymous meetings but often relapsed. When he relapsed, his wife would accuse him of not doing the "12 steps" well enough.

Victor said that he believed that his problem was related to an event in his teenage years when a man mistook him for a girl. He had previously been teased by other boys for having small features, after which he began doing different activities to become more masculine-looking, such as working out to developing big muscles.

When he was in his 30s, he had a sexual experience with a woman that made him feel "like a man." From that point on, he would seek out women for that first-time sex in order to experience that "like a man" feeling.

When Victor was asked to pinpoint the specific aspect of the sexual event that was most intense for him, he stated that his most intense feelings occurred when the woman would take off her clothes. At that point, he would feel "like a man" and be excited.

Victor's FS was the experience of feeling "like a man" linked with the behavior of watching a woman take off her clothes in preparation for having sexual intercourse with him. Again, it is important to note that sexual intercourse was not the goal of his behavior. Rather, it was the experience of feeling "like a man" that occurred before the actual intercourse.

                                       ImTT Press, publisher

Sexualizing of Objects and Behaviors

A person's pattern of bonding is developed in childhood. If the pattern of bonding is a loving interaction, then that pattern is activated when the adult seeks bonding through sex. If the bonding pattern is abusive, then the abusive/bonding pattern may be activated in sexual experiences. Whatever bonding pattern is learned in childhood, that pattern becomes sexualized when the adult seeks sexual connection.

This pattern-learned bonding applies to objects as well. When the adult seeks a sexual bonding connection, any objects that have become linked with the bonding pattern may become sexualized. If an object such as shoes or clothes are part of the bonding pattern, then when the adult seeks sexual bonding, the object may become a necessary part of the sexual bonding experience.

Learned Bonding in Childhood		Becomes Sexualized in Adult

Fetishes

A fetish is the result of an FS that links an object with a feeling. Wayne found cashmere sweaters sexually exciting. He had difficulty maintaining an erection if his wife wouldn't wear one when they had sex. Wayne presented for therapy because he had difficulty controlling himself at work if a co-worker wore a cashmere sweater, his wife complained about his not being able to have sex without her wearing cashmere, and his cashmere fetish making her feel belittled by his focusing more on whether she was wearing cashmere than on her sexual needs.

The question was obvious: "Why cashmere?" The answer to the question lay in his childhood.

Wayne remembered that his mother used to wear cashmere sweaters when he was a toddler. He had a vivid memory of the feel of the sweater and his mother's caress. This appeared to be the event that created the FS.

Breaking the link between the feeling of "bonding" and the the tactile feel of cashmere freed Wayne of his "cashmere" fetish.

Bonding Linked with Cashmere		Cashmere Linked with Sex

ImTT Press, publisher

Pornography

Pornography is simultaneously easier to treat and more difficult to treat than other compulsive behaviors.

Pornography is easier to treat because, with pornography, the person has identified exactly what excites him.

Just about anything is available on the Internet; so the person can find the exact pictures or action that excites him the most. Very likely, the person will have spent numerous hours discovering an exact enactment of that fantasy. This specificity of the fantasy makes the identification of the feeling-state easier.

Pornography is more difficult to treat because the person has to describe to the therapist what really turns him on. There is no such behavior as a "general" pornography addiction. Each person with a pornography addiction has a specific FS that must be processed in order to break the FS-created addiction. The identification of the FS must be exact. Identifying the FS requires the collaboration of both the client and the therapist.

As with all treatment, the therapist must be comfortable with the subject of treatment in order not to impede the client from resolving his issues. In addition, the client has to feel safe disclosing his pornography fantasy with the therapist. For both therapist and client, eliminating a pornography compulsion requires processing images that both may be uncomfortable discussing. Especially with sexual images, a good therapeutic relationship is essential for successful treatment.

The FS related to pornography can also be surprising. When Tom was asked to imagine doing his behavior from start to finish, he realized that the most exciting moment was when he put the search term in Google and was presented with many different choices. Which particular sex scene he watched was less exciting than the moment of choice. Tom's FS was the fixation of the "freedom to choose" linked with the different possible sexual scenes.

Barry's pornography compulsion began at 13 years old when he discovered his brother's "girlie" magazines. He began masturbating while looking at them. When he invited some of his friends over to also look at the magazines and masturbate, that made him the guy who had what all the guys wanted—for a few months, anyway.

He experienced feelings of being the "Big Man on Campus" and sharing a camaraderie with the other boys. Years later, Barry was still seeking these feelings by compulsively viewing pornography.

As Tom's and Barry's stories illustrate, it is important to keep in mind that, as with any compulsive behavior, what the person really wants is the feeling linked with the behavior. As with sex addiction, a pornography compulsion is not about the sex but about the feeling linked with the behavior.

Anger and Defiance

Anger problems result from two different psychological dynamics:

1. The first dynamic creating anger issues is the result of abuse. Abused people may become triggered into anger when some current event activates the old hurts. Resolving anger problems resulting from abuse requires processing the memories and images that are causing the anger.

2. The second dynamic creating anger behavior is an FS that links a positive feeling with the behavior of anger. Examples of these positive feelings are feelings of power, dominance, superiority, and righteousness. The linkage of the positive feeling with the anger behavior can be broken utilizing FS treatment.

Feeling-States Linked with Anger

Sam presented for therapy with problems of PTSD and anger issues. After four sessions, the PTSD symptoms were no longer present. However, he continued to have problems with anger, both at work and at home. When asked what positive feeling he had associated with anger, Sam replied, with intensity, "Righteousness." Using FS treatment, the linkage of righteousness and anger was broken.

In the next session, Sam reported that his anger had been greatly reduced but that he was still having some problems at home. When Sam was asked, again, what positive feeling he experienced when he was angry, Sam replied this time, "safe." For Sam, the behavior of anger made him feel safe. Again, the fixation between the feeling of "safety" and the behavior of anger was broken using FS treatment. Afterwards, Sam reported that he felt guilty and ashamed about his previous behavior.

Sam's anger behavior was the result of two fixated ASFs—righteousness and safety. Once those FSs were broken, the powerful feeling of intense anger was no longer a factor that interfered with his interactions with others.

Other forms of behaviors related to anger behavior are the behaviors of resentment and "holding a grudge"—both of which may be linked with ASFs. The holding-a-grudge behavior, for example, may be linked with a feeling of being "powerful."

In addition to being linked with ASFs, feelings of resentment and holding a grudge may be also be forms of pain avoidance. The grudge behavior, for example, may help the person avoid feeling the pain of losing, related to the winning/losing dynamic. For more on the winning/losing dynamic, see *Image Transformation Therapy* (Miller, 2015).

Anger and Combat:

The feeling of anger is often embedded in FSs in people who have experienced combat. During a firefight, anger is a natural reaction when people are trying to kill you or your buddies. The survival response in combat is to produce high levels of adrenaline, which creates an intense feeling of being alive. That "alive" feeling fixates with the anger experienced during combat and creates an FS. When the soldier returns home, that adrenalized anger can be activated by the slightest frustration.

Usually the anger is controlled, but the act of controlling the feeling takes tremendous

ImTT Press, publisher

effort. One soldier stated that what he liked best after releasing his anger fixation was that, for the first time, he could enjoy playing with his 4-year-old daughter. He no longer became angry when she did her normal "4-year-old little girl" behaviors.

Processing the anger related to combat is different from how one would process other FSs. With most FSs, identifying and processing the memory when the FS was created is the best approach. However, using the original event when the FS was created will not work with combat-related anger. The reason is that, at the time the FS was created, the client was in survival mode—the fight/flight reaction created the anger necessary for the fight response. That anger was necessary at the time. As a result, the client will resist any attempt to process the anger when focusing on the originating event because in that situation, anger was an appropriate and necessary feeling.

Instead of processing the combat memory, process a recent event involving the client's family, especially his children. Because the client will recognize the inappropriateness of his anger response with his children, the FS can be eliminated easily.

Feeling-States Linked with Defiance

The feeling of defiance is not an ASF. Rather, defiance is like the behavior of compulsive anger—there is a powerful positive feeling linked with the behavior of defiance. David had difficulty with authority. Even though he knew that breaking the rules would get him into trouble, he would break the rules anyway. He would justify his behavior to both himself and others by stating, "The rules are stupid." The feeling that Tom had linked with his defiant behavior was a feeling of power.

Another ASF often linked with the behavior of defiance is a feeling of a stronger sense of self. When a person is defiant, the behavior sets boundaries between the person and whomever he is being defiant towards. That boundary provides an "I am" experience. In other words, a person with a weak sense of his own self may be using defiant behavior to support his personality. In this situation, the images creating their weak sense of self may need to be released before the person will be willing to release the FS. To change these images, use Image Transformation Therapy.

Defiance can also be viewed through the lens of the winning/losing survival dynamic (Miller, 2015). Maintaining a feeling of defiance prevents the person from experiencing the pain of losing. Before eliminating the FS, release the pain of losing so that the person will allow the link between the positive feeling and the behavior of defiance to be broken.

Defiance can be treated using the fantasy image approach—that is, creating an imaginary scenario that resonates with the positive feeling related to behavior of defiance. However, the defiance dynamic may need to be processed, focusing on a specific person. Processing the fantasy image first may allow the person to gain access to the memory about whom the person feels most defiant.

> **Defiance is the behavior, not the feeling in the FS**
>
> **Example: FS = Feeling powerful + defiant behavior**

67   ImTT Press, publisher

Codependence

Codependent behavior has been a very difficult problem for therapists to help their clients resolve. Intelligent people, who rationally understand that their relationship with a particular person is unhealthy—maybe even dangerous—continue to seek a relationship with the person they should be avoiding.

What has been overlooked in the treatment of codependent behavior is the FS that links a desired feeling with either a type of person or a specific person. In either case, breaking the FS eliminates the codependent behavior.

Codependence linked with a specific person:

Sarah had broken up with an abusive boyfriend. Even after processing memories related to abuse and neglect from her childhood, Sarah's desire to be with her ex-boyfriend had not changed.

When Sarah was asked, "What was the most positive experience you had with your boyfriend?" Sarah, recalling that moment, stated that the experience happened when they were lying on the couch and he was holding her. "I felt this wonderful feeling of wholeness." Even though this "moment" lasted only a few minutes, an FS was formed that fixated the feeling of "wholeness" with her ex-boyfriend. Processing the FS broke that fixation. From that point on, Sarah no longer wanted to have anything to do with him.

Codependence linked with a specific <u>type</u> of person:

Some codependent FSs are focused on a specific <u>type</u> of person instead of on a specific person. For example, a person may leave one abusive relationship and then begin a relationship with another person that turns out to be also abusive. The events that caused this dynamic likely occurred in childhood. Albert had a number of relationships with women that were characterized by a pattern of the women withholding love and affection. What kept him in the relationships was that occasionally the women would give him the love he needed. The relationships would break up for different reasons, but his next relationship would be similar.

When Albert was a child, Albert's mother had a very similar interaction with him. She would withhold her love and approval for long periods of time and then, out of the blue, be very loving. Because of Albert's intense desire for a feeling of "bonding" with his mother, whenever she was loving, his reaction was intense—creating an FS that linked the feeling of "bonding" with "withholding" behavior. Thus, as an adult, Albert sought to have relationships with "withholding" women. Breaking that FS allowed Albert to find a relationship with a woman who did not withhold emotionally.

ImTT Press, publisher

Codependence and the Safety-FS:

Most codependent FSs can be easily resolved. Usually, the person already has a powerful reason to leave the relationship before seeking therapy. This reduces resistance to releasing the FS. However, when the FS involves the feeling of safety, the person may have a strong resistance to releasing the FS.

For years, Connie had been in an abusive relationship with her husband. She would leave him, stay away for a week or more, talk about divorce, and then go back to her husband. For a while, her relationship with her husband would be stable until his behavior became abusive again. Even though Connie was aware of this pattern, she couldn't stop herself from going home again.

The reason for Connie's behavior is that Connie's Safety-FS had created the leave-return behavior. Connie would leave her husband when he abused her. Then Connie would return to her husband when the Safety-FS overrode the memories of abuse.

When Connie was asked what was the most positive experience she had had with her husband, she said that, when they were dating, he protected her from a man who was stalking her. That he was now abusive and decidedly unsafe to be around did not alter the FS created during that event. Feeling-states, as described previously, do not alter with experience.

After the FS was identified, Connie expressed an ambivalence about releasing the FS. Connie's resistance to releasing the FS was the result of a feeling of terror resulting from the stalking incident. The person who was linked with safety was her husband. As long as Connie felt terrified, she was not going to give up what made her feel safe.

In order for Connie to release the FS linked with her husband, the feeling of terror had to be released first. ImTT was used to treat the memory of being stalked. After the memory was processed, Connie was able to release the FS easily and no longer had any interest in returning to her husband.

A codependent FS should be suspected when a relationship is either dangerous, abusive, or making a person miserable— in order words, painful—and the person doesn't leave. While economic difficulties and problems with domestic violence can prevent a person from leaving the relationship, the possibility of an FS should be investigated, especially if the person leaves and returns.

Co-Dependent Question:

What's the most positive experience you've ever had with...?

ImTT Press, publisher

Codependence and Sexual Fantasies

In the previous discussion of utilizing fantasies to identify FSs, fantasy was used to elaborate and/or articulate the feeling embedded in the FS. However, behaviors resulting from FSs may be more subtle than the usual types of addictions and compulsions. Fantasies can be used to uncover these more subtle patterns of behaviors.

Sexual fantasies can be a powerful approach toward identifying these more subtle patterns of behavior. The person may not act out the fantasy or may even be disgusted, revolted, or ashamed of being sexually aroused by the fantasy. Nevertheless, if a fantasy creates an intense sexual arousal, then the dynamics of that pattern will likely be acted out in some form in the person's life. The fantasy creates an intense arousal precisely because of the ASF embedded in the fantasy. Eliminating the link between the fantasy and the ASF will allow the person to make changes in his life often where the exact source of the dysfunction was difficult to identify.

Jane's Rape Fantasy

Jane had a rape fantasy. She fantasized about being dominated sexually, taken against her will. Most of the time, she wouldn't let herself think these kinds of thoughts; the fantasy was very ego-dystonic. Nevertheless, every now and then, she couldn't stop herself from "letting go." While Jane did not directly act out on this fantasy, Jane was attracted to men who were mildly dominating. She would eventually grow tired of this type of interaction and break up the relationship.

The feeling-state that Jane was acting out was the feeling of "safety" linked with the behavior of being dominated. She was only able to identify the FS because of the fantasy. In her real life, the behavior was not obvious. By identifying her secret fantasy, Jane was able to identify a subtle pattern of behavior in her life that was affecting which type of man she was attracted to. After processing the FS, Jane found that she began to be attracted to men who presented better relationship possibilities.

Vicki's "Servicing the King" Fantasy

Vicki was a 45-year-old female presenting for therapy because of a history of depression and anxiety. She had been married for 15 years to a man who was (most of the time) quietly controlling. Occasionally, when he didn't get his way, he would become loud and angry.

Vicki saw herself as a housewife whose job was to take care of her home and her husband. She saw her job as an act of service, which also fit into her religious views of husband/wife relations. Therapy revealed that Vicki had been dissatisfied with this arrangement and didn't feel that she was getting her own needs met.

At this point in therapy, many of Vicki's traumatic memories and codependent issues had been processed. She was speaking up for herself more than she had previously and was developing a more independent life. However, Vicki still became frightened when establishing boundaries. To identify the pattern underlying the anxiety, Vicki was asked to identify her secret sexual fantasy that was intensely sexually arousing.

Vicki described a sexual fantasy, set in Renaissance time, in which she was in the "service of the king." She would serve him by making his bed, bringing him food, and doing whatever needed to be done.

ImTT Press, publisher

In Vicki's sexual fantasy, she would be making up the bed and the king would come up behind her and undress her. She would not initiate any sexual action but would physically adjust to his needs. The most intensely arousing part of the fantasy was when the king would be surprised and delighted at her sexual response, realizing that he had found someone very special.

The psychological dynamic in Vicki's fantasy is that the king would recognize, through Vicki's service and response, that she was a "special" person. This dynamic had been playing out in Vicki's life by her continuing service to her husband and the denying of her own needs.

The fantasy was processed as an FS. Vicki then segued back to an event linked with her mother in which her mother made her feel that nothing she would ever do would be acknowledged or that she was in no way special and would never be. This event was processed with ImTT.

What is important to note is that Vicki's intense sexual fantasy originated in a non-sexual desire to be recognized and feel special. While Vicki's being-of-service behavior was also acted out in her life, in her church, and with others, the dynamic had also become sexualized.

Vicki's secret sexual fantasy was actually a window into the fundamental psychological dynamics that had had a major impact on her life by affecting her behavior with authority figures, including her minister, husband, and other authority figures. Instead of setting appropriate boundaries, in order to be recognized as special, Vicki would often not voice her opinion or ask for what she needed. Once this FS was eliminated, Vicki was able to "stand up" for herself and set appropriate boundaries.

Sexual Fantasies: A Window into Hidden Unmet ASFs

Jane's and Vicki's sexual fantasies revealed a normal human desire that had become sexualized. Jane wanted to feel safe; Vicki wanted to feel special. These desires had arisen out of their respective childhoods and had become sexualized when the women reached adulthood. These fantasies did not indicate some deep, dark twisting of their souls or horrible deformation of their personality that forever marked them as warped.

Rather, these fantasies reflected the unmet ASFs of childhood, normal human feelings that had become fixated with dysfunctional behaviors. As with any behavior resulting from an FS, eliminating the FS eliminates the behavior. As this discussion illustrates, sexual fantasies can be used to identify psychological dynamics that might otherwise remain hidden.

Sexual Fantasies

A window into our unmet ASFs,

Not **a window into our soul.**

---

71   ImTT Press, publisher

Obsessions

Obsessive thinking results from two different psychological dynamics— seeking a feeling or avoiding a feeling.

The difference is simple:

1. When a person is trying to change the outcome of what happened, the dynamic is "pain avoidance."

2. When a person is enjoying what he is thinking about, the dynamic is "wanting to experience a feeling" (a feeling-state).

Obsessive thinking results from:

1. Pain Avoidance: Trying to change the outcome of a situation. ("woulda, coulda, shoulda" thinking)

2. Feeling-State: Seeking a feeling.

ImTT Press, publisher

1. Avoiding-pain obsessive thinking:

Avoidance-obsessive thinking occurs when a person is attempting to change the outcome of a situation. The person is doing "woulda, coulda, shoulda" thinking—trying to avoid the pain or fear of the actual outcome by thinking of behaviors that could have changed the outcome of the situation.

Pain-avoidant obsessive thinking is eliminated by processing the memory or feeling that the person is avoiding.

The following is an example:

Charles

Behavior: Charles had lost a lucrative contract that would have made him the top salesman in his company. Charles thinks about this event every day, sometimes for hours, trying to figure out what he did wrong and what else he could have done to change the outcome.

Psychological dynamic:
What Charles is trying to do is avoid the emotional pain of failure by re-thinking the event. Whether there was anything he could have done to change the outcome is not the point. The obsessive thinking is caused by the need to change the outcome so that he will not have to feel the pain of what actually happened.

Solution: The solution is to get Charles to release the pain so that he does not have to fight off the feeling of pain by trying to create a different outcome. Use Image Transformation Therapy to release the image and pain of his failure.

2. Positive-feeling obsessive thinking

Positive-feeling obsessive thinking occurs when the positive feeling becomes linked with an imagined scenario. A person may fantasize about something that happened in the past such as the former high school quarterback described below. Another possibility is that the person may completely make up the scenario such as fantasizing about dating a celebrity. This obsessive type of thinking is driven by a positive feeling that has become linked with the obsessive thoughts. Use the FS protocol to eliminate the FS causing the obsessive thinking.

The following are examples of obsessions caused by an FS:

A 40-year-old man who is constantly thinking about the football touchdown he made in high school that won the homecoming game because it makes him feel like the "Big Man on Campus,"

A woman who spends hours trying to re-create how she looked when she won the beauty pageant thirty years before because it makes her feel like a "winner."

The combat veteran who plays Tour of Duty for hours a day because he re-experiences the adrenalized excitement of combat.

All these people suffer from obsessions resulting from FSs. The consequence of these obsessions is that these people are focused on the past instead of the present and future. Locked onto the past, their psychological energies are not available for current use. Feeling-State treatment allows the person to focus his energies on creating accomplishments in the present.

73

ImTT Press, publisher

Food Compulsions

Compulsions linked with food include behaviors as varied as binge eating, general overeating, and addictions to sweets or carbohydrates. As with other compulsive/ addictive behaviors, behaviors regarding food must first be evaluated for which behavior is being activated—the avoidance of a feeling or the seeking of a feeling.

A common avoidant dynamic regarding food results from the feeling of being overwhelmed. A common hiding behavior for people who feel overwhelmed is to come home from work and watch TV and eat at the same time. If the food compulsion appears to be the result of avoidant behavior, use the Image Transformation Therapy approach for releasing the feeling of being overwhelmed (Miller, 2015, 2016).

The first person with whom the author used the FS treatment for a compulsive food behavior had a compulsion to eat a large pizza all by herself. As Ricki was about 150 pounds overweight, eating large pizzas was a problem. When Ricki was asked what she felt before beginning to eat her first slice of pizza, she replied that she imagined that everyone in her family was taking a piece of pizza. At the end of the processing session, Ricki did not think anything had changed; so that weekend, she ordered a large pizza. Ricki was only able to eat about two-thirds of the pizza and became nauseated. Much to her surprise, Ricki couldn't eat the entire pizza as she had always been able to do previously.

Stephanie's eating problem centered on McDonald's. Every week she felt compelled to eat at McDonald's at least once a week, usually on Friday. This behavior was not a major problem in her life, but the behavior was disturbing to her because she wanted to eat healthy food, not fast food. However, Stephanie could not stop herself from going to McDonald's every week.

Stephanie remembered that her grandmother used to take her to McDonald's every week for a treat. The feeling she identified with the McDonald's experience was "bonding." Once the FS was eliminated, Stephanie was easily able to stop eating at McDonald's and find her "bonding" experience elsewhere.

Jeff's difficulty with eating was that he was constantly eating unless doing other activities that kept him busy. The type of food did not matter as long as he was eating or drinking something. Jeff appeared to have an "oral" fixation. Jeff was able to identify that his eating behavior was linked with the feeling of "belonging." For Jeff, eating reminded him of the times when he and his mother would have a special meal together— a meal that she had cooked especially for him.

An FS of Intergenerational Joining can also cause overeating. Debbie's mother was overweight. She would often say to herself that she was just like her mother— overweight. In all other ways, Debbie felt that she was not like her mother at all. Debbie was able to begin losing weight when the FS of the image of being overweight was broken from the feeling of connection with her mother. Eating was just a means of attaining the self-image of being like her mother so that she could feel connected with her mother.

ImTT Press, publisher

Substance Addiction

Substance addictions are often composed of both psychologically induced FSs and Sensation-FSs. For some people, for example, cocaine can produce such an intensely euphoric experience that an FS is created. This "high" or Euphoric-FS is usually one of the common reasons for relapse. In addition to the Sensation-FS, a psychological FS may also need to be eliminated. For example, people with alcohol addiction often have an FS related to the ASF of belonging or "fitting in." Both sensation and psychological types of FSs will need to be eliminated.

Treatment for both psychological and Sensation-FSs is similar, in that the most intense FS is eliminated first. Using the metaphor presented previously, the "brightest light" FS is the focus for treatment. For substance addictions, the Sensation-FS is often the most intense.

The good news for treating the Sensation-FS is that the Sensation-FS is usually the easiest to identify and process. People suffering from substance addictions usually have a vivid memory of the first and/or most euphoric time they used the drug. The intensity of the vivid memory, the "chasing the dragon" memory, makes identifying the most intense FS easy.

The other piece of good news about the Sensation-FS is that the Sensation-FS is the easiest and fastest to process. Because the Sensation-FS is created as a reaction to the drug and not an underlying emotional need, there is no underlying trauma or negative cognition to process. After processing the Sensation-FS, treatment moves on to process other FSs or avoidance issues related to the addictive behavior.

The challenge of treating the Sensation-FS is that the person may not want to become activated into that feeling. Rogert had been successfully controlling his desire to use cocaine but was still having problems with cravings. The idea that he would have to allow himself to experience the euphoric sensation in the session, even if lightly, made him afraid of relapsing.

Therapists also have difficulty with this—afraid that their client will relapse after the session. Therapists' fear of clients' relapses because of possibly becoming activated in session can be an obstacle to eliminating the Sensation-FS.

A solution to the problem created by the fear of relapse from experiencing the Sensation-FS is to reduce the intensity of the FS by using the Euphoric Sensation Release Protocol (ESRP). Using the ESRP, the person can reduce the intensity of the "high" or "rush" sensation so that the memory or image can be more easily processed.

Eliminating the FS removes an important cause of relapse

ImTT Press, publisher

Abstinence or NOT
For Behavioral Compulsions:

For behavioral compulsions, an important difference between the FS treatment and other forms of treatment is that abstinence is neither necessary nor desired for successful treatment. FS treatment requires that the person, at least, lightly, tune into the feeling embedded in the FS. People who are abstaining from performing the compulsive behavior may resist experiencing the feeling. If the person resists tuning into the feeling, the FS will not be eliminated. The people who have the most difficulty with experiencing the ASF are those who have successfully controlled their behavior and are afraid to experience the feelings that are linked with previously relapses.

In addition to being able to easily tune into the feeling, when a person's behavior is out of control at the beginning of therapy, progress in therapy can easily be evaluated. The feelings and behavior that arise between therapy sessions indicate areas that still need to be targeted for treatment. In addition, progress in therapy can be easily tracked as the person's behavior changes.

The result of a successful FS treatment of behavioral compulsions is that the out-of-control behavior is no longer out of control. In fact, the compulsive gambler can gamble, the compulsive shopper can shop, and the sex addict can have sex—all without losing control. The goal of FS treatment for behavioral compulsions is not abstinence but normal, healthy behavior.

discuss releasing the feelngs of boredom, emptiness, and the panic thst they cant have the addictive behavior. as necessaey for addictive behaviors in general.

Abstinence or NOT
For Substance Addictions

Substance addictions pose a more complex picture than behavioral addictions when considering abstinence. Clinical experience suggests that different substances may necessitate different treatment procedures.

Cigarettes, for example, can continue to be smoked while treatment is proceeding without interfering with treatment. As the FSs related to smoking are processed, the client's frequency of smoking is reduced until they have completely stopped smoking. The taste and smell of cigarettes becomes less and less appealing until the smoker cannot stand the taste and smell. Because of the health risks of cigarettes, clearly, the goal of treatment is abstinence. However, the behavior of not smoking should result from the elimination of the FSs that cause the urges and cravings to smoke. This makes it easier to discern when the smoking addiction has been resolved.

On the other hand, the use of intensely stimulating drugs such as cocaine, amphetamine, and heroin during treatment may interfere with the processing of the FSs. There has not been enough clinical experience of FS treatment to make any definitive statement of whether using these drugs during treatment interferes with treatment. There have been positive indications of the effectiveness of FS treatment in an in-patient setting.

Clinical experience with alcohol suggests an even more complex dynamic. Alcohol use can be significantly reduced and eliminated even while the person continues to use alcohol—a process that is similar to cigarettes. Some people appear to be able to use alcohol socially after the FSs are resolved. However, the long-term use of alcohol after the FSs have been eliminated has not been sufficiently studied to understand the risk of generating another addiction to alcohol.

While in some people, alcohol addiction appears to be the result of psychological FSs, other people's alcohol addiction appears to have a more physiological basis. Clearly, for those people, abstinence is necessary.

For most substance-using behavior, continuing to use the substance is unhealthy. We know from experience that relapse is common, even expected. Eliminating the FSs removes an important cause for relapse. Whether the FSs are caused by psychological issues or a Sensation-FS, eliminating the FSs eliminates powerful positive memories that make relapse more likely.

Another bit of possible good news in regard to relapse for drug addiction is that, once the Sensation-FS is eliminated, using the drug again does not appear to re-create the FS. While this is not definitive yet, reports indicate that, when the substance is used again, the intensity of the feeling that created the FS is not present.

These reports are congruent with the concept of the "down regulation" of the receptor sites for the drug—the tolerance effect. This might mean that eliminating the Sensation-FS for the drug may have long-term implications that alters the course of behavior when a person relapses—the person who relapses may have an easier time returning to sobriety instead of having to hit "rock bottom" again before seeking treatment.

ImTT Press, publisher

Addiction and Avoidance Behavior

Avoidance of feelings is often an additional problem for people who have behavioral and substance addictions. For example, a person whose problems at work are causing anxiety may drink to avoid those feelings by "drowning their sorrows." This is a separate issue from the addictive behavior that the FS treatment focuses on. In this situation, FS treatment will not resolve the problem.

FS treatment targets a feeling that the person wants to feel, not a feeling the person wants to avoid. When a person is doing the behavior in order to avoid a feeling, the appropriate approach is to process the memory or feelings that the person is trying to avoid. Then the person will just stop doing the behavior.

Dan began drinking after his wife left him. He had not had a problem with alcohol previously. However, after the breakup, the only way he could go to sleep was to drink. Otherwise, his pain, rage, and his obsessively thinking about her would prevent him from sleeping.

Because Dan's sleeping and drinking problems began after the breakup, it was clear that Dan was using alcohol to avoid his emotional issues. Processing Dan's pain and rage allowed Dan to return to his previous level of alcohol use.

For many people, however, addictive behavior often does double-duty. The behavior is used for both obtaining the desired feeling (an FS) and for avoidance as well (e.g., not feeling depressed). Therefore, both dynamics will have to be targeted. Which dynamic should be worked on first depends on the situation. A person whose depression precedes his addictive behavior may have to have the depression treated before eliminating the FS.

A clinical evaluation is necessary to determine the appropriate course of treatment. Treatment may begin with FS treatment and then segue to treating the issues the person is attempting to avoid feelings about. Once that issue has been resolved, FS treatment can be resumed.

On the other hand, treatment may begin working on issues causing the avoidant behavior and then segue to FS treatment. It all depends on what is "present in the room" during the sessions.

ImTT Press, publisher

Chapter 6
More Case Studies

Pornography Addiction

The following case is an example of resolving a behavioral addiction without targeting the initial event. It was only after the addiction had been resolved that the client remembered what event the FS was connected with.

The case also presents an example of how the ASF (excitement) can be linked with a negative feeling—in this case, humiliation. The challenge for processing the FS was for Terry to identify and then experience both the feeling of sexual excitement and the feeling of humiliation at the same time.

Feeling-States

1. Humiliation-sexual excitement + looking at a specific type of pornography

2. Bonding with father

Terry's Story (in his own words)

I gradually developed a porn addiction, with a specific fetish for interracial pornography, especially involving fantasies of humiliation. It started at a previous job at which I looked at various types of porn on the Internet after hours when nobody was around. I noticed feeling disturbed when I read accounts of Japanese women who were attracted to black men.

I changed jobs and looked at pornography less there because there was a strict policy against the abuse of the Internet, it being a government facility. But I did look a couple times, at risk of getting caught, and became interested in interracial pornography.

ImTT Press, publisher

Later I bought my first home computer and started to look at porn sites a lot when I was home, including the interracial sites. Later I left my job, but the interracial fetish was really starting to affect me. I remember that, when I went out in public, I was always looking for interracial couples, specifically a black man with a white or Asian woman, and wondering about them.

I started to have long sessions looking at pornography, and gradually it became almost all interracial porn, looking at a couples site that catered to that type of fantasy. These involve fantasies of a white husband giving his wife to a black man and being humiliated in front of the black man. I could spend hours on this fantasy, many times a week.

I felt this was bad for me and tried to limit it several times, but each time I would forget and get drawn back into looking at it on the computer. Sometimes I would look at other types of porn, and then it would draw me right into the interracial porn.

In therapy, the therapist used the FS approach to deal with the interracial fetish. After a couple rounds, I had a childhood memory of being humiliated by my mother. I was in my bedroom with my brother and a female friend who I liked a lot. I was about 5 or 6 years old, and she was a year or two older. We were daring each other to do things, and my brother dared me to go into the closet and close the door. I did that, and as a joke, I dropped my pants and opened the door. My mother just happened to walk into the room right then, and when she saw me, she yelled and scolded me to put my pants on. I was humiliated in front of the girl and my brother.

After we processed this event, I didn't really have as strong an interest in interracial porn. I looked at it a few times but wasn't drawn into long sessions with it. But I did still feel addicted to porn in general and felt "out of control." A thought or picture of a woman would trigger me to go to the computer and start looking at hundreds of pictures. I also started paying for porn on cable TV.

I decided to try an FS session on myself, first bringing up the desire to go over to the computer and then just started the eye movements. I brought up a memory of my father showing me pornography when I was about 8 years old. He showed me his magazines in the workshop, while he wore his bathrobe and masturbated. What I noticed was the feeling of bonding with my father, something that was otherwise somewhat lacking at this point of my life. I began to concentrate on that feeling in the FS and went a few more rounds.

Since then, pornography has not been a compulsion for me. Before, just looking at one picture or video would usually cause me to lose control and indulge in it for hours. But now I can look at one thing and stop myself right after. I can also prevent myself from starting if I decide to.

Discussion: This case presented a specific challenge. Most of the feelings connected with FSs are positive feelings that people enjoy feeling. However, in this situation, the sensation of sexual excitement was connected to the feeling of humiliation. The consequence of the sexual excitement being connected to humiliation was that Terry did not want to let himself experience the complete FS—it was too humiliating. The result was that, in the first session, targeting the FS did not result in a complete resolution. Once this process was explained so that Terry understood why he had to experience the entire FS, the FS was quickly eliminated.

ImTT Press, publisher

Codependence: Unable to Let Go of a Relationship

Cindy: FS = safety and security + her relationship with her ex-husband

Cindy was a 42-year-old Caucasian female with a history of alcoholism that had been exacerbated by her fear of depression.   Cindy's problems with depression had increased since her divorce seven years previously.   Her depression had been so intense after her divorce that she was terrified of it happening again. Whenever even the hint of depression surfaced, Cindy would drink.

Cindy's childhood had been one that involved intense feelings of lack of safety and security.   When her husband told her that he loved her, the feelings she experienced were intense feelings of safety and security.   When Cindy felt the need for safety and security after her divorce, she was compulsively drawn back to that memory and feeling-state.   Since she could not connect with him because of the divorce, she became depressed because she could not experience the feelings of safety and security, which she so badly wanted.

Cindy's difficulty was that, as abusive as her marriage had been, she was still unable to let it go; she remembered the good times that she would never experience again. When these memories were activated, she would feel depressed, wanting the relationship she could not have—and then she would drink.

When Cindy was asked what the most positive experience was that she had had with her ex-husband, she remembered an event in which he said, "I love you." Cindy identified that FS at a PFS = 9. After three sets of EMs, the PFS reduced to 0.

The next session, the FS remained at PFS = 0. Cindy reported that she felt ready, for the first time since her divorce, to move on with her life and was looking forward to the future with optimism.

A Forbidden-Exciting Relationship

Jeanette: FS = Excitement (danger) + ex-boyfriend

Jeanette's difficulty was that she was engaged and living with one person while still having an attachment to a previous boyfriend.   She had broken up with him because he did drugs and lived a very dysfunctional life. Nevertheless, being with him had been exciting and thrilling. He was the adventure she wanted instead of being the "good girl."   This feeling-state of forbidden excitement and sex linked to the ex-boyfriend had been fixated at the beginning of their relationship when they did drugs together and had sex.

Her other relationships after that boyfriend seemed, in her words, "dull" because her excitement was linked to the ex-boyfriend. After she had broken up with him, she continued having a sexual relationship with him between other boyfriends.   Even while living with her current fiancé, she would sometimes still have sex with her ex-boyfriend. Jeanette entered therapy because she loved her fiancé and wanted to have a good marriage with him.

Using the FS treatment to break the FS linking excitement with her ex-boyfriend enabled Jeanette to have a deeper, more intimate, relationship with her fiancé.

Impersonating a Police Officer and a Sex Addiction

Jim:

FS1 =
Behavior: Impersonating a policeman
                        +
ASF: "Getting Over"

FS2 =
Behavior: Impersonating a policeman
                        +
ASF: "Winning"

FS3 =
Behavior: Sexual behavior
                        +
ASF: "Getting Over"

FS4 =
Behavior: Sexual behavior
                        +
 ASF: "Victory"

Jim's Story (In his own words)

I grew up in a household of five kids with both parents still married. I am the fourth child.   Throughout my childhood, I was in and out of trouble in grade school. I first had the "rush" and "accepted" feeling when I came in contact with the police at age 12. The officers supported me and at times gave me tools such as a toy police badge and T-shirt that aided me in becoming a "police" addict.

I started to love this feeling when I realized that I had an initial surge of power, assurance, and a strong sense of belonging. At age 14, I continued this path of playing the cop. However, the police were concerned about me no longer being a child. And, as a result I was arrested for the first time at 14 for impersonating a police officer after I stopped some lady who ran a stop sign.

This "rush" (the feeling of power, assurance, and a strong sense of belonging) led to a compulsion that continued for well over 10 years. Over this course of time, I had been arrested over 7 times by various agencies for impersonation. I spent almost a year in a youth correction center, then half a year in county jail for this disease.

Even after being punished, I continued on the path of impersonating. I acted out by telling random strangers, to actual police officers, to making false police ID cards, purchasing police-style shoes, radios, and even an old police car. This became a part of my daily routine, which was leading me in the direction of disaster. It was obvious that I was powerless over this illness and that no amount of medication could solve this matter. Furthermore, there aren't any "impersonation anonymous" meetings, and the resources were pretty limited.

FS Treatment:

In addition to impersonating being a policeman, Jim was also having problems with a sex addiction. He was always trying to seduce women he had never had sex with previously. Once he had had sex with a woman, he moved on to the next one.

The "impersonating a police officer" compulsion was treated first. Jim identified the FSs "getting over" and "winning." After 2 sessions of treatment, Jim reported that he no longer felt any urge to lead people to believe in his being a police officer or to ask for professional courtesies from police officers.

The sex addiction FSs were similar to the impersonating FSs. The FSs were "getting over" and "victory." After 2 sessions of treatment, Jim's urge to seduce women had vanished.

82   ImTT Press, publisher

Instead, several weeks after eliminating the FS, he came into the session saying that he now no longer knew how to relate to women; since he was no longer trying to seduce them, Jim was at a loss as to what to say. After a few sessions of helping him develop new socializing skills, Jim was finally able to interact with a woman as a friend instead of as only a target of his seduction.

Gambling and Socializing

Tim:

Tim had two compulsions: gambling and the compulsion to socialize or to be with people in a social setting.

Gambling

Tim's gambling compulsion was to play the lotto. Tim would spend $20-$30/day every day of the month. In addition, he would organize a lotto pool in his workplace and buy the tickets himself.

Tim's Gambling ASFs:

1.   Winning

2.   Belonging

3.   Freedom

The Winning FS was his winning feeling.

.   The Belonging-FS involved his feeling part of a group. In this case, the group was betting on the lotto together.

The Freedom-FS was the feeling of being free to do whatever he wanted.

Result: After processing the FSs, Tim stopped buying lotto tickets on his own, he no longer got the lotto pool together, and he only bought $2-3 worth of tickets each week with the office pool.

Socializing

When Tim initially came for treatment, he said that people had told him that he had an alcohol problem because he was at a bar every night of the week. When questioned about exactly how much he was drinking, he stated that he was only drinking two beers each night, spaced out over 6 — 7 hours.

Tim's actual compulsive behavior was going out to restaurants and bars every night, usually around 5 p.m., setting up everything. He would go to a particular table at his favorite restaurant and control the TV on sports night. The table was usually reserved for him most of the time. He would stay at the restaurant for a few hours, then go to two other places over the course of the evening. On weekends, he would arrive at the restaurant by 2 or 3 p.m., long before anyone else would show up; he was always the first to arrive.

It became apparent that Tim was going to these places to socialize. He would talk with people for hours. Tim's compulsion wasn't to drink but to socialize.

Tim's Socializing ASFs:

1. Belonging

2. Importance

The Belonging-FS focused on being part of a group of people who got together at the restaurant.

The Importance-FS focused on how he felt being the central person who got things together each night.

After processing the FSs, Tim began working out after work and only went to the restaurant after 7 p.m. On weekends, he would show up in the late afternoon if there was a game on but had stopped being the first person to arrive.

An Addiction to Figuring Things Out —A Virtue Turned Into a Vice (In her own words)

In my case, I'm addicted to figuring things out in the field of behavioral health. It all started with the prerequisite intense desire for the feeling of being smart and understanding mental health. These intense desires were created by my family always calling me a "dummy" and them having mental health issues that were toxic to me.

Then I had the positive event—a eureka moment 10 years ago when my experimental data from an animal model of depression coalesced into a new theory of depression. I could literally feel waves of pleasure flowing throughout my body— I was high on the feeling that "I'm a genius!"

Ever since, I have felt compelled to spend more and more of my time working on figuring out other problems in mental health—what's going on neurobiologically and psychologically in psychosis, ADHD, PTSD, and how to increase delivery of effective mental healthcare. I keep doing it despite the fact that I haven't figured out a way to get rewarded monetarily for pursuing it and despite the fact that there wasn't as much interest when I published my depression theory as I expected and despite the fact that I'm neglecting my relationships. Now that I see what's going on by recognizing the match to the scenario you discovered, I've set up an EMDR session with a local therapist for next week.

Anyway, I'm telling you because I hoped that you might derive some benefit from seeing that your scenario is also valid in this unique circumstance where my behavioral addiction was to a kind of virtue rather than to a typical vice.

ImTT Press, publisher

A Complicated Addiction of Gambling and Sex

The following case illustrates some of the twists and turns of addictions that reveal themselves as the therapy progresses. The surprise for me was that Jon's addictions involved behavior that created arousal (which was expected) but also behaviors that caused relaxation.

Jon's Story (In his own words)

I started gambling when I was a small boy, when I was no older than 8 years old. I would make wagers with my older brother for chores around the house. We would place bets on the outcome of sports and video games. I lost most of the time, which made me want to bet even more. I soon felt the exhilaration and excitement of the games increase as the size of the bet was increased. I was hooked very young.

I made my first trip to a casino in Laughlin, Nevada, when I was 18. I was on my way to Marine Corps boot camp, and my mom and I went to have some fun. It was exciting to walk into the casino. The first thing I noticed was the sound of the slot machines. Then the smell of cigarettes and stale beer hit me and the music of clicking chips as people nervously shuffled them in their hands. I was in love; I had found a home.

My first bet in a casino was on a nickel slot machine. That was not enough action or risk for my blood, and I headed for the blackjack table. I think I lost a grand total of $40 my first trip. The feeling I had in that casino is one that will haunt me for a long time; I had the itch and wanted more. It was not an obsession, not yet. My life was far from normal. I was a ferocious drinker and in trouble often while in the Marines. I was discharged from the Marine Corps honorably for a medical condition after serving two years as a presidential guard for Presidents Reagan and Bush.

I landed a job making okay money, and the calling of Vegas was stronger than ever; I had to get back.

I made my first trip within 2 months of being discharged from the Marine Corps. I was soon married, and my wife and I made a trip to Vegas every few months for the first 2 years of our marriage. The trips to Vegas were not enough to quench my appetite for action; I had to have more. Soon I was betting on darts, golf, and everything in between. Of course, I was making small wagers with my friends, but the excitement was enough to make even a boring game a matter of life and death. As a salesman on the road, it was not long until I found the card clubs in Los Angeles, and I began playing poker. I started out in the small games, playing $1-2, 7-card stud. I was not very successful but never wagered more than $20-$60 at a time. It was manageable, but it was something I hid from my wife. Thus began the excitement of a secret life and playing for small amounts held higher stakes than winning or losing. I had to win or risk being found out.

I began to run into trouble with my drinking and was distracted from playing for a while, maybe a year or so. When I decided to stop drinking and start playing cards, things went from bad to worse. I would play between 2-4 times a week, depending on my schedule and how much time I could get away from the house.

My wife and I owned a dance studio with her parents. She would work until 9 or 10 at night. I would get home from work around 5, and she would be at work. It was plenty of time for me to make the 45-minute drive to the casino and wager my usual $40 in a small stud game. The games were crazy for me to play because I had a time limit of a few hours and had to force my hands; if I lost, I risked being found out.

ImTT Press, publisher

I soon began to chase losses and would borrow money from friends and family to cover my bets. It was never much money -- a few hundred here, fifty there.

I was good about paying the money back; so not many questions were asked. My life was beginning to become a lie. I was playing more and more. Then it happened; I won my first jackpot. It was not much—close to a thousand dollars—but no one knew I had won the money. Now I could play undetected and move to bigger games. I lost that thousand in a day. I chased that thousand with 3 thousand, and I lost. Now the trouble started because that was my rent money and I had to tell my wife what happened.

As I look back at the time in my gambling career, I see how much time I wasted. It was not just the time at the tables; it was the time chasing the lies and all the energy I spent remembering what lie I told and to whom. All the energy wasted on trying to figure out how I could get more cash so I could get back into action. I can remember the day Magic Johnson announced he had HIV, I was sitting at a 4-8 stud game. I was 23 years old. Gambling for me was something I had to do, and I had already spent close to $10,000 doing it. I had to find new friends because the people I grew up with were sick and tired of watching me get crushed at the casinos. The hardest part was the horror of leaving a casino after losing money I did not have. It was to the point where I was considering suicide. Of course, all of my troubles were because of a bad marriage. No way was I sick or to blame. I had never even heard of Gamblers Anonymous.

My marriage ended badly. It ended because she was married to a compulsive gambler who would tell a lie if the truth suited him better. I moved out to live with a friend. Of course, the first trip we took was to Vegas.

To finance that trip I sold my car that I did not own. The bank made a mistake and sent me the pink-slip. I sold it for $950. I lost a lot of money I did not have that trip and spent a long time paying people back. I stopped gambling for a long while and consumed myself with a heavy dose of cocaine, beer, pot, and Ecstasy. I snapped out of that after 14 months. I was tired of not having money and just dreaming about it.

I was fueled by a desire to be a big shot with lots of money and power. I found just the job to do it in. Coming off a long run of drugs, I had enough energy to become successful quickly. Not only was I clean, I was back and soon found myself married to an intelligent, wonderful woman. I was promoted several times rapidly and began to make serious money, in the 6-figure range.

Now I could go to Vegas and be the big shot I always wanted to be. Oddly enough, I did not go that often, maybe 4 times in the first year. The second year I went 8 times. Then it happened; I crossed the invisible line of compulsion, and it became an obsession. I had to go to Vegas. I soon was going every chance I had, not to mention the high stake poker games I would get into with my friends. It would not be uncommon to win or lose several thousand dollars in a night. I was full steam ahead with my compulsion, and so was my career—I was making more money than I ever had and had gotten into some favorable stock positions.

I had a chance of a lifetime present itself to me. I left my career of 4 years and went to work for an Internet company. I received stock options and soon became a day trader, augmenting that action with my gambling. I was wagering money 12 hours a day. I forced an idea and created an opportunity to move to Las Vegas and open a wireless Internet company. My wife, who was pregnant at the time with our child, did not want to go.

The fights were nasty, and I was to blame. I wanted Vegas more than her and more than my unborn child. I had to be in the action. Finally, I got my way; she agreed to move to Las Vegas. I had close to $1 million in stocks and cash when I went out ahead of my wife to scout around for a place to live. One of the first weeks I was in Vegas, I was staying at the Hilton and won close to $10,000 playing blackjack. I had started with $300. I knew I was going to take Vegas apart. I was living my dream, staying at different hotels on the strip, living in suites, working during the day and gambling all night long.

I would wager between 5 and 15 thousand a week, playing craps, blackjack, and 3-card poker. It was an incredible feeling to walk into a casino and have people know my name. I enjoyed the VIP treatment and could not stop. My wife and I started fighting about my gambling long before she moved to Vegas to join me. She knew I was in trouble with my gambling but had no way of knowing how much money I was actually losing. I would lie to her, and she believed me. Before she moved to Vegas, I swore off gambling forever.

It was not long before I was back at it again, playing as hard as ever and betting more and more. I checked myself into an out-patient program for compulsive gamblers. I went 5 days a week 3 hours a day. That lasted for a month. I was back placing bets within 1 week of leaving that program. I would go to a Gamblers Anonymous meeting, then to a casino. I was spending cash at an incredible rate.

By this point my daughter was born, and I was a poppa. I swore gambling off again and knew I was in trouble. My obsession to play was stronger than any promise I made to my wife, daughter, or god. I had to be in action at any cost. I would send my wife back to California so I could play. She had control of the bank accounts, the ones she knew about.

I was in action full time and playing in the casinos between 4 and 8 hours a day. It was costing more than money; I was losing precious time with my new daughter and wife. I would tell her I was going to the store and stop at the casino and place a few thousand dollars in bets within 30 minutes to an hour. It finally became a problem so immense that I agreed to leave Las Vegas. I had squandered my entire fortune at this point except for maybe a hundred thousand dollars

I took a job in Los Angeles. We sold our house in Vegas and moved in with her father, to save money. I promised to attend GA meetings and never to gamble again.

I did attend meetings for the first 2 months. The obsession to play was so great that it consumed me. I was back at my old company and had the autonomy to be gone all day. I was good at my job and was able to perform well with only a few hours a day of effort; that left me 8 hours a day. I started gambling again.

Within 3 months, I was back playing poker. This time my level of excitement was raised so that I had to play in the big games. I started playing Texas Hold'em and was playing $20-40 and up to $40-80 games. I blew through the rest of my money; I was broke within 18 months. I had spent close to a million dollars in a casino or in the stock market. All of it was gone.

My home life had deteriorated to the point of a constant fight. She did not believe a word I said and was right not to. I could not even believe myself at that point. I did not want my daughter to be exposed to the ugly fights, and I wanted to gamble when I wanted without my wife bothering me.

I left my wife and daughter so that I could gamble more. I spent the rest of everything I owned; I hawked art, my wedding ring, my watch—anything I had of value I either sold or hawked to play.

ImTT Press, publisher

I had gone into business with a friend and was borrowing money from my company faster than I could pay it back. I was at my wit's end.   The final straw came when I got an eviction notice for my apartment. I knew I was going to die if I kept up this pace. The amounts of drugs I had to ingest just to look at myself in the morning were alarming. I went to GA and surrendered. I had nothing left; my lease was up at my apartment. I had no way to pay rent. I was going to be homeless. A friend I made in GA took me into his house. There was 1 condition: I could stay rent-free as long as I did not place a bet. I went to work for my family and was working a program in GA. I made 103 days without placing a bet. I thought I had it licked. Little did I know. I started gambling on what would have been my 104th day of abstinence.

I had done things I never thought I would do to play cards. I wrote several thousand dollars in bad checks, I stole money from my family, my company, and my friends to play. I went on a 1-week bender that cost me over $10,000 I did not have. I lost my place to stay and was suicidal. My friends and family had had enough. I did not know what I was going to do. I checked myself into a rehab. I started working a program in the 12 steps of recovery. I was crazy.

I met Robert Miller while I was in recovery. The result of the FSAP is astonishing. I have no desire to gamble whatsoever. It has been lifted completely. I attend GA meetings regularly. The distinction for me is the fact that I do not have the compulsive desire to gamble. The thought to gamble has traveled through my mind without being a thought that I have to act on. I am able to let it pass through, where before I would have to act on that thought or call someone in the program to help me through that situation.

My thoughts of gambling do not have the energy they had prior to utilizing the FSAP.

FS Treatment:

What Jon didn't write about was that, in addition to his gambling addiction, Jon also had a sex addiction. Both of these addictions had some unexpected complications. During treatment, it turned out that Jon had two poker-playing addictions and two sex addictions. Jon played high stakes poker and low stakes poker. His total loss over 10 years was $1 million. Jon's sex addictions involved both going to strip clubs as well as massage parlors. These addictions had cost him over $100,000 during the course of 10 years.

The Feeling-States were:

Gambling

High Stakes Poker

1. Excitement: the danger of losing a lot of money
2. Importance
3. Winning

Low Stakes Poker

1. Belonging

Sex

Strip Clubs

1. Power
2. Importance

Massage Parlors

1. Intimacy
2. Connection

Jon's Results:

Strip clubs compulsion: stopped going to strip clubs and spending money.

High-stakes poker & Low-stakes poker: no longer felt compelled to gamble.

Massage parlors compulsion: stopped going to massage parlors

ImTT Press, publisher

Chapter 7

Transcripts of Therapy Sessions

The transcripts are divided into two sections. Section 1 utilizes the FSIP & ImTT protocols for processing feeling-states and traumas. Section 2 utilizes a combination of the P/TRP and the FSAP.

Whichever processing protocols are used, the sessions illustrate the process of identifying and processing feeling-states.

TRANSCRIPTS UTILIZING THE FEELING-STATE IMAGE PROTOCOL

TRANSCRIPTS UTILIZING THE FSAP AND P/TRP

Transcripts:

Utilizing the Feeling-State Image Protocol

Don: Smoking Marijuana Linked with
the Reward Feeling-State

Don has had a longstanding addiction to smoking marijuana. The feeling-state linked with smoking marijuana is the feeling of being rewarded. The FS is processed with the Image De-Construction Protocol (Phase 3).

Dr. Miller: All right. Entitlement—tell me what you mean by that.

Don: This week the peak of the heat wave—I think it was Wednesday—I just felt like it was hot. I was working all day, and I was sweating. I felt like I deserved a little something for me. I deserved to go home and look at pornography, or I deserved to maybe go to a massage parlor because I'm working hard, my back hurts, and I deserve it. When I get that way, it's very hard to get out of it because I started going down the funnel. I start to give in a little bit.

"Yeah, you're right, I do deserve that because it's for me. I do work hard, and she's not going to do anything for me."

But I didn't act out, and I didn't go look at porn. I used my phone list and called a brother. That's what it was like. It was, like, "I get to do this for me because I work hard and I deserve it." It was almost the same for pot too. I felt that was the same thing for weed too. I went with my buddy, who went to lunch. I like hanging out with him; so we went to his truck.

Dr. Miller: What is it that you deserve? Forget the content because, clearly, it doesn't make any difference whether it's weed or whether it's pornography. In other words, what is the feeling? You deserve what feeling?

Don: It's almost like I deserve an escape. I deserve to do something to make myself feel relaxed or do something to make myself feel better.

Dr. Miller: I think there's a feeling there that you're seeking more than just relaxation. You're feeling deprived in some way.

Don: Sure—well, not deprived—I guess you could call it that.

Dr. Miller: What would you call it?

Don: I don't know that I'd call it deprived. I feel like I earned it. It was, kind of, a reward.

                                       ImTT Press, publisher

Dr. Miller: A reward.

Don: Yeah.

Dr. Miller: That's what I think we're dealing with now.

Don: I feel like I need to be rewarded for my hard work other than a paycheck.

Dr. Miller: Reward is about approval. In other words, if you're growing up and your parent gives you a gold star, that's the reward.

Don: Yeah.

Dr. Miller: Your behavior is being approved of. Approval at that age is very intense. It has its own kind euphoric high in itself. Does that make sense?

Don: Yeah, it makes sense. I'm trying to think. It does make sense, given the way I was raised.

Dr. Miller: Well, the problem is that it's precisely the way you were raised that means that, when you've got rewarded even once, it would be really, really, really intense.

What's happening is that you're looking at different ways of feeling a super intense reward—whether it's pornography, whether it's—whatever else. The more intense your need for reward means the more you didn't get it. When you finally did get it, it becomes a really, really big, intense feeling. Then you start looking for it everywhere.

Don: I get it.

Dr. Miller: If you'd gotten a lot of approval from your parents to begin with, then reward wouldn't be that big of a deal. You're not hungry when you've been fed nicely. It's when you've been starved and then you finally get that meal that it's a really big deal—"Oh, my God, this is fantastic"—when it might be ordinary if you'd have just been eating regularly.

That's how feeling-states are created. There's a buildup for a desire so that, when you finally get it, it's really intense.

Don: Yeah, I understand that.

Dr. Miller: I want you to pick the behavior that is most rewarding.

Which of those behaviors is most rewarding?

Don: Pot.

Dr. Miller: Pot. Okay.

Don: Yeah, right now. Right now.

Dr. Miller: Is there a particular memory when smoking pot was really rewarding?

Don: Yeah, I can think of one.

Dr. Miller: Now, what I want you to do is hype up the memory and make it even more intense. I don't want you to feel it, necessarily, but I want the image to be that you've got three pounds of pot here—whatever it is that heightens that image that makes it feel that it's a reward.

Have you got it? Now see that image as being as being composed of tiny, tiny, tiny, little particles. Just nod your head when you get it.

Don: [Nods]

Dr. Miller: Now deconstruct the image. Let me know when you're finished.

[Pause]

Don: Okay.

Dr. Miller: Re-image it again, and tell me what you've got.

Don: Still the same old; I seem happy.

Dr. Miller: Now deconstruct the image. Let me know when you're finished.

[Pause]

Don: Okay.

Dr. Miller: Re-image it again and tell me what you've got.

[Pause]

Don: I have a blue background. I have to concentrate really hard to start even building me in the image. My bong is going, and the weed's gone. Almost my whole room—it's like blue, almost a blue box.

Dr. Miller: How does it feel to you?

Don: Relaxing. It's just like a cool, blue, mellow color.

Dr. Miller: Re-image it again, and tell me what you've got.

[Pause]

Don: Nothing.

Dr. Miller: Now we're going to release the pixel-particles of the old image from your body. Breathe into the center of your brain and see the particles going right out the center of your forehead.

Don releases from the body the pixel-particles of the image.

Dr. Miller: How do you feel?

Don: When I'm thinking about the entitlement, it's not a reward. It's weird. I have to think about putting myself in that place again. I don't think I want the weed; it's just that I want to do something to relax myself—or something for me.

What I have been doing—because I've been clean for a while—not for a while—for, like, a month and a half—a long time for an addict—I've been meditating. When I get home from work, I just find my quiet time. I used to either smoke pot on the way home or go in the bathroom and look at porn. I needed to do something to replace that behavior. I think that's more what I'm feeling now. I want to do something healthy.

I do work hard, and I should feel like I need to be rewarded, but I don't think I need to be rewarded with drugs or pornography as much as doing something healthy for myself, like taking 10 minutes and just going to a quiet place in the house and meditating and, kind of, clearing my mind through the day.

That's all I was doing with pornography, and pot was just smoking away my problems I had during the day. That's what I feel. It's weird because, when I think about getting home from work and—that's what I would do even before I would shower and—I would smoke pot and watch porn—I still feel like I should get some kind of reward, but I think that it should be more of, like, a healthy reward—something that's not going to hurt myself or my family.

Dr. Miller: Now what you're really talking about is you still need to feel approved of. You want to get approval for all you've done. Why do you need to be rewarded? Why don't you just do it because you want to?

Don: I don't want to. I do a job that I don't want to do.

Dr. Miller: What you do want to do is relax; right?

You don't have to be rewarded in order to relax. You can just relax because you want to.

Don: Meditate just because I want to?

Dr. Miller: That's right. It's not about whether you deserve it or not. It's about what do you want to do, okay? If you want to relax, fine. If you want to eat, fine. It's what you want to do.

The truth of the matter is that, when you break the link between reward and marijuana, you actually don't want to smoke it. Because smoking marijuana doesn't help your life. The question just becomes, "What do you want to do?" You don't have to justify going home and relaxing.

That's what you're, kind of, doing—"I worked hard; so I deserve this."

No. If you want to do it, just do it.

Don: Yeah, I get it.

Dr. Miller: Let's go back to the entitlement. How does that feel to you now?

Don: The entitlement? I'm thinking about—in a way, when I feel—it feels silly, in a way, that I would feel the need to reward myself for doing what most people do every day. A lot of people go to jobs they don't like.

My job isn't even really that bad. I just don't like being out in the heat and stuff. That's the only crappy thing about it.

It's more gratefulness that I have a job or that I have a job that provides for my family, rather than "Well, I have to go to this job and, since I have to go this job, I should get something for it." It feels like I'm thankful for this job.

Dr. Miller: Pretty big change in attitude?

Don: Yeah. Interesting.

If I really think about getting off from work, it doesn't seem that bad because my car is air-conditioned. I'm thankful for that. I live next to the ocean; so it's not that hot and I can always go swimming. I really have a lot more to be thankful for than feeling like I deserve something or feeling like I need to be rewarded.

Does that make sense?

Dr. Miller: Yeah, it does.

Don: I think a lot of it was—especially with the pot—a lot of jealousy, in a way, because a couple of my co-workers smoke pot, and I get jealous because of it. Not "jealous," but— because I know that it's not going to help me—it's not going to help my life at all—but it's still, like, jealous that they can do it, even though that—I can see that it's not helping them at all. It's, like, "Man, I wish I could do it," but—I think about all this stuff.

Dr. Miller: Now, when you think about that, do you still wish you could do it?

Don: No.

Dr. Miller: That's what you've been feeling in the past?

Don: Yeah.

Dr. Miller: In the past, you've also identified pot with reward. Now that we've broken the link between pot and reward, you'll see the difference.

When you really let yourself think about it, how does it feel now?

Don: When I really put myself in that situation, getting off of work, it doesn't seem appealing. It doesn't seem like I should feel the need to do something.

There's more of a gratefulness that I get to go home to a family and my wife. If I did smoke pot, nothing good comes out of it. I'm more happy—I'm happier without it than with it. That seems clearer than it did before.

Now it's more like I don't want to do it and I'm not thinking of, "Oh, I wish I was high." It's the opposite. I think about all the stuff that comes with being high—all the negative stuff that comes with being high and then—"I'm just not doing it."

We'll see how it goes. The next week will be interesting.

Dr. Miller: We're through for the day, and we'll follow it up.

Don: Okay.

Next session

Dr. Miller: How's it been?

Don: It's been really well, as far as, I haven't had any real urgency. I've thought about it, but after that I'm, like, "I'm obsessed over it." I just haven't had a big pull towards it like it was, which is very amazing because it was a big part of my life. It was bothering me for a long time that I may not be able to smoke. Who knew? Look what happened. [Laughs]

I can't explain it. On the other hand, it almost feels like I really don't want to do it anymore. I haven't replaced it with anything. I haven't been drinking excessively or anything weird like that—maybe a beer a night that I drink.

ImTT Press, publisher

Don: Pornography Addiction Session

In addition to his marijuana addiction, Don also has a long-time addiction to pornography. This behavior is processed with the FSIP.

Dr. Miller: Just describe what your addictions are—the behaviors.

Don: Well, marijuana. Yeah, I smoke pot. I started when I was 17. I've pretty much smoked on and off since I was 17. I'm 31 now.

My sex addiction started with pornography when I was younger. As soon as I turned 18, I started going to strip clubs, discovered peep shows. That became my main inner circle behavior until I was around 22. Then I started going to live shows where I was actually in a room with a woman while she was undressing. Then from there, I went to a lot of porn. I got married, had a kid. I still watch porn, even though I've been caught several times by my wife—told me I had a problem—I denied it.

Then when I was—four years ago—probably 27 or 28—I can't remember—I started wanting to go to massage parlors. That's when I got caught the first time. That's what brought me to SAA. I went to SAA for a while, never did the steps, struggled, couldn't get more than three months of sobriety within a time before I looked at porn or went to a peep show.

Then recently—I mean by, like, a year ago—I started going to massage parlors. The massage parlors just sucked up a lot of money. My wife found out. I would go to two meetings a week. I've been sober for 60 days. Well, that's sober from my sex addiction. Pot—I just can't seem to care. I just keep going back to it.

Dr. Miller: Tell me about your upbringing, your childhood.

Don: About when I was 7, one of the older neighborhood girls would coerce me into their little back shed area and physically touch me. She would talk me into touching her. She was probably 12 at the time, and I was 7.

Dr. Miller: At that time, what did you think about?

Don: I just thought it was weird. I didn't know why I liked it or why I was doing it.

Dr. Miller: Did you like it?

Don: Yeah. I didn't know why or I didn't know what exactly I was doing, but I have this curiosity about women and their bodies. I think that's what led me to porn.

Dr. Miller: When you think of that event—and there are numerous times; right?

Don: Yeah.

Dr. Miller: What do you think of it? Does it feel exciting?

Don: At the time, it was exciting. Now, when I look back on it, it makes me feel bad because my innocence was lost right there at 7. Even though I know she was a kid and I was a kid, we didn't really know what we we're doing. I don't feel good about it now. I don't feel, "Oh, yeah."

                                                                       ImTT Press, publisher

Dr. Miller: What age did you start watching porn?

Don: I started around 11. I knew my dad had a stack of Playboys. Whenever I was left home alone, that's the first thing I would go to is the Playboys. For two or three years, I would just look at them. Then I finally figured out that I could masturbate to them. Masturbation felt good.

Dr. Miller: When you came home in the afternoon, how long would you do it for?

Don: If I was home alone, I would do it until I orgasmed.

Dr. Miller: No, even before then. Even before the masturbation began.

Don: Before—probably 40 minutes to an hour because I didn't want to get caught— I would keep it real short because I knew, if I got caught, my dad would hide them somewhere else.

Dr. Miller: All right. To you, 40 minutes to an hour seemed short?

Don: Yeah.

Dr. Miller: It's pretty clear that your pornography addiction began, you said, at age 11; right?

Don: Mm-hmm.

Dr. Miller: You came home and you're all alone and—it's very clear that you had a pretty neglectful childhood.

Don: Yeah.

Dr. Miller: They may have been hitting you, but that might have been the most touch they ever did—not a lot of "I love you"'s and "You're wonderful"?

Don: Yeah, there wasn't a lot of that.

Dr. Miller: Is there any particular kind of porn that you looked at? Was it just women? Was it women having sex? What exactly was happening on the porn?

Don: It was women having sex, but it was more of women being seduced or women being the seducer.

Dr. Miller: Women being the seducer?

Don: Yeah. I like the women being the strong one—the strong come-ons. Then there was a lot of MILF porn.

Dr. Miller: A lot of what?

Don: A lot of MILF porn. Like moms. My mom's best friend or something along those lines.

Dr. Miller: Do you see how this connects with that little 11-year-old girl when you were 7?

Don: No. No, not really.

Dr. Miller: She was the controller. She was the older woman who was taking you along and doing this to you.

Don: Oh, wow.

Dr. Miller: Her touching you and you touching her was, likely, the most gentle, loving, caring touch you were probably used to having. Of course, it was sexual, but, you know, it was touching. It was being touched in a nice way. It felt nice at the time anyway; right?

Don: Mm-hmm

ImTT Press, publisher

Dr. Miller: What would be that feeling? Did you feel connected? bonded? cared for? What is it that you would say was that feeling?

Don: I think it was more of a feeling of acceptance.

Dr. Miller: Acceptance. Okay.

Don: Because there was someone there who wanted to touch me in that way. I felt like I was finally given what I wanted. Even with the massage parlors or having sex with my wife or those girlfriends before that, it was more of I can feel they love me and I feel they accept me for who I am. Like, I know the massage parlors—they get paid to do it, but there's still that feeling I get of, you know—

Dr. Miller: You may know it's nonsense, but the feeling is there anyway.

Don: Right.

Dr. Miller: It's what's called a feeling-state. So you've defined what you want from porn and from massage parlors as the feeling of acceptance.

That's what's going on. It's not about sex. It's about that you've got the feeling of acceptance at 7 years old, in a sexual situation; and you keep recreating that same thing time after time after time. Think how powerful that need for acceptance must be. You're finally getting it.

Every child needs to feel powerfully accepted; right?

Don: Right.

Dr. Miller: That's what you're doing. It's not about sex. It's about feeling accepted. If you would have felt, with your parents, that feeling of acceptance, then the thing with the little girl would have been just probably a pleasant interlude that you don't think about too much. That would have been it. It wouldn't have changed your life. As it was, it changed your life because you finally got what you were looking for—acceptance.

Don: The more I'm thinking about it now, the more it makes sense because I was always trying to get it from my step-dad to my step-mom to my dad. I was always trying to be accepted. I want to be a part of the family or—I don't want to feel like the odd person out. The more that I'm really thinking about it now, the more I think it's been a driving issue. It's, kind of, crazy because I always thought it was just something that I did and there was really no reason for it.

Dr. Miller: No, there is a reason for it.

Addictions are always caused by very powerful reasons—feelings that we really, really powerfully want. That's why it overrides all sensibility, all rationality, is because, at a most primal level, acceptance is a fundamental need. We need to be accepted.

Don: There has to be a family unit to survive.

Dr. Miller: Exactly, as a matter of fact. Without acceptance, we die. Now we're going to break apart the feeling of acceptance from the behavior of watching porn.

Don: Okay.

Dr. Miller: What's the most powerful memory you have of sex and acceptance? It could be the memory when you were 7.

Don: I don't know. There are a lot of memories. The most recent one was I would go to the massage parlor in Oceanside and there's this beautiful girl that I'd always get a massage from. We always got along, and we always had a nice conversation, and it came to the point where I really looked forward to just—not the sexual part of it, not the massage part of it—just talking to her. I felt like I can connect to her and I felt like I wasn't judged. Sometimes I feel like my wife judges me a lot on the things I say because I say some pretty awful stuff without thinking about it a lot of time. I was able to, like, say stuff that I normally wouldn't say to my wife and her accepting and maybe laughing at it or something. I think that's, like, the most recent one. I think that's probably the most powerful one too.

Dr. Miller: I'm going to ask you to—now, in order for this to work, you're going to have to really get into the feelings, which you probably have done everything you can to avoid— but in order to process it so we can clear the feelings totally, you have to be willing to get into the feelings.

Don: Okay.

Dr. Miller: What I want you to do is to really get into that memory and the connection with sex. Just close your eyes and really get into it and, when you get just as intense as you can, open your eyes—or, actually, just nod your head. Don't open your eyes, just nod your head. On a 0-to-10 scale—a zero is you don't feel anything and 10 is super, super intensity— what number would you put it at?

Don: I'd say an eight.

Dr. Miller: Where do you feel it in your body?

Don: My heart is beating fast.

Dr. Miller: Now, I want you to see that image you have as composed of tiny little pixel-particles, okay?

Don: Okay.

Dr. Miller: Now deconstruct the image.

Don deconstructs the image and releases the pixel-particles with the IDP.

Dr. Miller: When you think of the connection between acceptance and that woman, how does that feel to you now?

Don: That was a little less—a lot less-er.

Dr. Miller: What number would you put it now?

Don: I'd probably say a "one." I don't feel as anxious or my heart beating fast.
I feel a lot calmer.

Dr. Miller: Scan your body. Is there any tension or any anxiety anyplace in your body?

[Pause]

Don: No. I feel pretty relaxed.

[Pause]

Dr. Miller: Imagine you're going to a massage parlor. What comes up for you now?

Don: Wasting money [laughs], for one. That's a big one. When I think about that particular girl, I can see the illusion I put on it and the illusion of this acceptance I put in there. I definitely see a lot of wasting money.

Dr. Miller: Now we're going to do something a little different. Can you feel the fact that you're not accepted? Does that feel painful or fearful to you?

Don: Fearful.

Dr. Miller: What color is that terror?

Don: It's definitely black.

Dr. Miller: Where is it located in your body?

Don: I feel the same way, but I feel, like, in front of my head.

Dr. Miller: Think of the black as being composed of tiny little particles, and breathe into those black particles and breathe them directly away from your body.

Don releases the black particles of terror with the P/TRP.

Dr. Miller: How does that need for acceptance feel now?

Don: It feels calmer. It's still fearful that I might not get the acceptance, but I feel more along the lines of "I'm not going to die if I don't get what I want," to—where I was before, it was, like, "If I don't do this, I'm not going to feel right."

Now, when I think back or I think about that I'm not getting any acceptance, I know that it feels more of "I'm still going to survive another day."

Dr. Miller: What's the fear about now?

Don: The fear before was that I won't be accepted at all. I guess I still have a little fear that I might not get accepted.

Dr. Miller: Which will mean what? Which would just be painful?

Don: It would just hurt, but it won't—

Dr. Miller: Won't kill you?

Don: Yeah.

Dr. Miller: What color is the pain?

Don: Red.

Dr. Miller: Where is it located? See the red as composed of tiny little particles of red, and breathe into the red particles, and breathe them right out your body.

Don releases the red particles of pain with the P/TRP.

Dr. Miller: Think about being accepted now. How does that feel to you now? Or not being accepted, how does that feel?

Don: It's weird. I feel better about it. I feel like—it's kind of, hard to put it, but I do feel like I cannot—when I think of not being accepted by my wife or by a person at work, I feel better about the situation.

If I went home today and I asked my wife for sex and she says no, I don't think my reaction would be to go act out with porn. Because that's normally what it would be. Sex means she didn't accept me, so I'm going to go get it somewhere else.

I really feel that I don't think I would do that today. I think I would be okay with it. For the most part, I have really—since she discovered me, I've been pretty good about not acting now.

Dr. Miller: You've been controlling it?

Don: Yeah, I've been—

Dr. Miller: What we're trying to do is make it so that you don't need to control it. If your wife says no tonight, what's your reaction? Let yourself really think about that.

[Pause]

Don: I think it'd be okay. I think it'd be more like a Beatle's song, just *Let It Be*—it is what it is—and I'll just go do something else.

Dr. Miller: Ever felt that before?

Don: Not really. No. It's been more of a "Bullshit. I guess I'll just have to go do something else." Not like now where it feels more of like I can just go do something else. Not like I have to. That feels good. Jesus. [Laughs]

I feel like I'd be in a safer place if she said no. It's still weird because I still—a part of me thinks that I might always have that feeling of fearfulness of not being accepted and —maybe that's just, like, my addict just trying to hold onto something.

Dr. Miller: No. Look, you've had the expectations about that all your life. It's going to take a while for you to realize you're not responding the same way. Okay?

Don: All right.

Dr. Miller: Let's try and take this a step a further. Is there a negative belief you have about yourself that makes you feel like you can't be accepted?

Don: Yeah.

Dr. Miller: What's that?

Don: It's more of a—I always think I'm going to be a fuckup in some way or another. I'm always going to do something self-destructive to screw up my life because that's been my MO for a while now.

Dr. Miller: If you're always doing something self-destructive, what does that mean about you?

Don: I think it means that, in a way, I want to self-destruct because I'm always looking for something to hurt myself in some way.

Dr. Miller: In other words, do you think you're a fuckup?

Don: Yeah.

ImTT Press, publisher

Dr. Miller: Is there some particular memory that you have, that, when you think about being a fuckup, that's the memory that pops up for you?

Don: Mm-hmm.

Dr. Miller: What's that?

Don: When I was 13—12 or 13—I think I was 13—I was in 8th grade or 7th grade— and we used to bring home these progress reports. They were like—they weren't grades—"This is what—you are on your way. If you keep f'ing this up, this is what you're going to get."—I got a C in English. I was always a pretty good student. I always got A's and B's. So I got a C, and I remember thinking, "Well, C is not that bad. I did some passing. I'm an average kid," and—I remember bringing it home and my stepmother just, fucking, flipping out, like beyond all belief, because it was a C.

"How can you do this? I thought you were smarter than this. This is how you start deteriorating your life and, if you start getting C's now, you'll get C's forever and you'll never amount to anything."

In my mind, it was just so blown out of proportion. I didn't know what was going on. My dad came home, and he did the exact same thing—well, my dad was a truck driver; so he was gone every other day—he did the exact same thing. I remember him, really, like, getting down on me, telling me that I'm a screwup and that, if I keep this up, I'll be a fuckup my whole life.

Dr. Miller: What I want you to do is picture this event. What's the most intense part of this memory?

Don: My stepmother looking at the progress report in the car and just feeling her initial anger. I could just feel it in the car. I think that's the most—

Dr. Miller: The thought is "You're a fuckup."

Don: Yeah. My thought is "I just did something really bad."

Dr. Miller: "I just did something really bad." And that means you're a fuckup.

Don: Yeah.

Dr. Miller: It's that feeling; right?

Don: Yeah, that feeling's exactly it.

Dr. Miller: On a 0-to-10 scale, how intense is this?

Don: I'd say it's a 9.

Dr. Miller: Where do you feel it in your body?

Don: I feel a lot of stress in the back of my head. That's where I feel a big buildup.

Dr. Miller: What I want you to do now is close your eyes, think of this event. Think of the intense part of the event and that you're a fuckup. Your stepmother, is she yelling at you yet?

Don: Yeah.

Dr. Miller: She's yelling at you. She is calling you all kinds of stuff, really putting you down, "You're a fuckup."

Don deconstructs the image and releases the pixel-particles with the IDP.

101   ImTT Press, publisher

Dr. Miller: Any particles left in your body? Any tension left your body? On a 0-to-10 scale, when you think of that event, how intense is it for you?

Don: I'd say it's a 2.

Dr. Miller: It's a 2?

Don: Yeah.

Dr. Miller: Okay.

Don: It feels a lot calmer, and just the fact that I know now that it was—because I always knew that it was an overreaction, but it was just that feeling—it's the feeling of these people who are supposed to love you telling you that you're a screwup. It's just hard to handle. But I feel better about it because I know that I am not a screwup.

Dr. Miller: That's about what I was going to ask you.

Don: I know that I am not a screwup. I mean—

Dr. Miller: The 2, what's the 2 about?

Don: Just because—like there's still some resentment just because—it's, like, they couldn't fucking understand that I was a fucking kid?

Dr. Miller: You're angry with them.

Don: Yeah.

Dr. Miller: Okay.

Next Session

Dr. Miller: Good afternoon, It's been a while now.

Don: Yeah, it has been a while. Odd, interesting stuff I've noticed, as far, like, when my wife wouldn't want to have sex with me or just when I didn't feel, like, accepted by her—so I've noticed that has gone away a lot.

It's really weird for the first couple of times it happened. Not only that, but the wanting to look at porn, that's gone away too. It was really weird for first four or five days because I realized I didn't want to and I didn't understand why I didn't want to because usually it's a struggle almost every day.

Don:
Avoidance Behavior Urges After Processing the Feeling-States Linked with Pornography the Previous Session

This session takes place after a previous session in which the feeling-states linked with Don's pornography compulsion have been processed. At the beginning of the session, Don discusses his homework of repeating his previous behavior in order to discern if any other feeling-states are linked with the behavior. No feeling-states were identified as being linked with his current behavior. Instead, the images underlying Don's avoidance behavior are processed with Image Transformation Therapy.

Even though FSs are not processed in this session, this transcript is presented to demonstrate how treatment for addictive behavior can change from processing FSs in one session to processing images creating avoidant behavior in the next session.

Dr. Miller: How have you been doing?

Don: I'm doing good. I looked at porn, like we talked about. Probably about five minutes in, kind of, got this feeling of like, "Why am I doing this?" I just really thought about like, "I could be having sex with my wife right now if I really wanted to."

When I finished—because I was already in the middle of everything—I didn't feel I needed to go back to it the next day. I didn't feel any compulsion to start again. It felt good. Especially when I had that, "What am I doing? I could get the real thing if I wanted to." It was a good exercise. I'm glad I did it because I didn't feel any pull towards it the next day or any big urge to do it.

The only time I really feel like doing it—when I get that urge—is when Susan won't have sex with me. I don't think it's a good thing to be, just, "She's not going to have sex with me? Then I'm going to go look at naked women. That will show her." That's what's going through my mind. I don't think that's healthy.

Dr. Miller: You've been feeling kind of defiant. It's like, "I'll show her."

Don: Yeah. It is what it's always been when she didn't want to have sex, "Well, I'm going to do what I need to do." That always led to me doing it more compulsively and all that.

Dr. Miller: This time it didn't happen?

Don: No, it didn't happen.

Dr. Miller: Good. Let's go to the image of her not wanting to have sex with you.

Don: Because it happened—not this Tuesday, but last Tuesday. I was coming home early from work. She had just put the baby to sleep. She texted me.

She's, like, "Oh, I just put the baby to sleep"—you know—"When you come home, please be quiet."

I was, like, "Well, I'll be home in 20 minutes"—you know—"Let's have some adult time. Let's have some sex."

She didn't say yes or no. So when I got home, I was expecting to, and she was studying for her midterm. She was, like, "Well, no, I'm not going to do that. I'm in the middle of something."

So I was kind of bitter.

Dr. Miller: What makes you bitter?

Don: Because I expected it when I came home. I expected her to be in this mood that I thought that she was going to be in, even though she said that she didn't even confirm that she was ready to have it—or ready to have sex with me. I built all these expectations up in my head, and then nothing got met. Then I felt like my needs were not getting met because my expectations weren't getting met.

Dr. Miller: How did that make you feel?

Don: It made me feel like my feelings were hurt, made me feel like she didn't care about me. That's a big thing.

Dr. Miller: What's that image of her not caring about you?

Don: The image?

Dr. Miller: Yeah. What would that look like?

Don: I don't know. Just her—like me telling her that I like—that I need something from her and then her walking away. That would be an image.

Dr. Miller: You think?

Don: Yeah.

Dr. Miller: When you think of this image, is it painful?

Don: Painful.

Dr. Miller: What color is the pain?

Don: I don't know. I guess it would be red.

Dr. Miller: Where's it located?

Don: It's, like, here; or it's here (indicating).

Dr. Miller: See the red as being composed of tiny little particles. Breathe into the particles and breathe them directly out of your body.

Don releases the red particles of pain with the P/TRP.

Dr. Miller: How do you feel?

Don: The more I think about it, I always know that it's just a little voice that I have, telling me that she doesn't love me and that the only way a person loves you is through sex—or they can show you they love you is through sex. I know that's not true.

Now when I think about it, it doesn't seem so reinforced. It doesn't have the power it once did.

ImTT Press, publisher

Dr. Miller: Do you still have the image of Susan walking away from you? Is that what it is?

Don: Yeah.

Dr. Miller: What happens is that the image gets triggered and it triggers pain. We've reduced the pain, which means that it doesn't have the power it used to, but the image is still there. Now we're going to deconstruct the image. See that image.

Don: [Nods]

Dr. Miller: Now pixelate the image. Tell me when you've got it.

Don: [Nods]

Dr. Miller: Now deconstruct the image. Tell me when you're finished.

Don: [Nods]

Dr. Miller: Re-image it again. Tell me what you've got.

Don: It's still there.

Dr. Miller: Now pixelate the image. Tell me when you've got it.

Don: [Nods]

Dr. Miller: Now deconstruct the image. Tell me when you're finished.

Don: [Nods]

Dr. Miller: Re-image it again. Tell me what you've got.

Don: It's not her at all.

Dr. Miller: Now pixelate the image. Tell me when you've got it.

Don: [Nods]

Dr. Miller: Now deconstruct the image. Tell me when you're finished.

Don: [Nods]

Dr. Miller: Re-image it again. Tell me what you've got.

Don: Nothing.

Dr. Miller: Now we're going to go to the body and release the pixel-particles of the image. Okay?

Don: Okay.

Don releases from the body the pixel-particles of the image.

Dr. Miller: How does that seem to you now?

Don: It doesn't seem painful. It seems more adult-like, I can handle it like an adult. It's not how I usually handle it, which is leaving the bedroom, pouting about it.

It feels better.

Dr. Miller: Now we're going to look at it in a different context. One of the most powerful forces is survival. One of those of survival forces has to do with winning and losing. When you lose, it's like you're losing your chance of survival, survival of the genes. When you can't have sex with Susan, it's like you're losing. Does that make sense?

Don: Yeah.

Dr. Miller: When you think of her saying "no" as meaning that you're losing, what does that feel like to you?

Don: It's more like a self-esteem blow than anything else because it's like she doesn't want me for some reason, not that—she can tell me, "I just don't feel like it" or "I have a lot of stuff going on," but it's as if she doesn't want me, and that hurts my self-esteem.

Dr. Miller: That means you're losing; right?

Don: Yeah. That means, if I was in better shape or if I did something right yesterday or something like that, then she'd want to have sex with me.

Dr. Miller: You would win then. If you had done something different—looked better, whatever it is—you would win. As it is, you lose.

Don: Yeah.

Dr. Miller: Does that feel painful or fearful?

Don: Painful.

Dr. Miller: Painful?

Don: Yeah. It's a self-esteem blow. It hurts my self-esteem.

Dr. Miller: It's hurting your self-esteem, but self-esteem has a lot to do with—when you win, you have high self-esteem; right?

Don: Uh-huh.

Dr. Miller: When you lose, what happens?

Don: I have low self-esteem.

Dr. Miller: Exactly. What we're going to do is clear the pain of losing; so it's no longer about that. Because in life, sometimes you win, sometimes you lose. That's just the way it is. What we do is, when the pain of losing gets to be intense, we can have urges to do things—or we can get angry or something like that—in order to not feel like we're losing, instead of just saying, "Okay, well, that was one round. Next round will be there tomorrow. No big deal."

But it triggers a very intense pain of losing, which is a very big deal. What we're going to do is then process that pain of losing. What color is that pain?

Don: It's like a yellow. Like a yellow color. It's not like a red, which is weird. When I think about losing, it's a yellow.

Dr. Miller: Where is it located?

Don: It's up in my gut, right here (indicating).

Dr. Miller: See the yellow as composed of tiny little particles. Breathe into those yellow particles, and breathe them directly out.

Don releases the yellow particles of pain with the P/TRP.

Dr. Miller: How does that feel now?

Don: When I think about it, it doesn't feel painful or fearful. I don't know. When I think about it, it just feels like I can deal with it.

Dr. Miller: It what?

Don: It feels like I can deal with it a lot more grown-up now.

ImTT Press, publisher

Dr. Miller: What's the image of losing?

Don: Image of losing for me? I don't know. It makes me think back to when I played lacrosse, when we lost. I get that image of me standing there with my lacrosse stick, just looking all "down."

Dr. Miller: Is it a powerful image of losing?

Don: No, not really. I'm trying to think. It's—me alone is a powerful image because, really, that's what it would come down to. If I lost everything, that would be losing my family and stuff. Then it would just be me alone.

Dr. Miller: Now see it composed of tiny little pixel-particles. Let me know when you've got it.

Don: Okay.

Dr. Miller: Now deconstruct the image. Let me know when you've finished.

Don: Okay.

Dr. Miller: Re-image it again. Tell me what you've got.

Don: I see myself. I know it's me because of the outline. I see my outline, but I can't see details of my body or face.

Dr. Miller: Pixelate the image again. Let me know when you've got it.

Don: Okay.

Dr. Miller: Now deconstruct the image. Let me know when you've finished.

Don: Okay.

Dr. Miller: Re-image it again. Tell me what you've got.

Don: I can't tell. It's just blurry.

Dr. Miller: Pixelate the image again. Let me know when you've got it.

Don: Okay.

Dr. Miller: Now deconstruct the image. Let me know when you've finished.

Don: Okay.

Dr. Miller: Re-image it again. Tell me what you've got.

Don: It's just foggy.

Dr. Miller: Pixelate the image again. Let me know when you've got it.

Don: Okay.

Dr. Miller: Now deconstruct the image. Let me know when you've finished.

Don: Okay.

Dr. Miller: Re-image it again. Tell me what you've got.

Don: I'm not there, almost like a blank slate.

Dr. Miller: Pixelate the image again. Let me know when you've got it.

Don: Okay.

Dr. Miller: Now deconstruct the image. Let me know when you've finished.

Don: Okay.

Dr. Miller: Re-image it again. Tell me what you've got.

Don: Nothing.

Dr. Miller: We're going to run through the body again and clear out the pixel-particles of the images, okay?

Don: Okay.

Don releases from the body the pixel-particles of the image.

Dr. Miller: What do you feel now when you think of that image?

Don: It doesn't have that much power. Especially when I think about it, especially when I think about sex as a winning or losing thing, it doesn't seem all that bad. I didn't really lose anything, especially now that I think about it. You can't really lose something that's not there in the first place.

It makes me feel again like when I got that feeling with the weed, how I wasted a lot of time and energy sweating over something that I really didn't have to worry about all that much. That's how I'm feeling now.

Dr. Miller: We're just going to do some changing patterns, a little bit. What I want you to do now is just think of Susan for about 15 seconds. Think of going home to her tonight. Nothing particular, just there you are, saying, "Hello." [15-second pause]

Tonight, think about wanting to have sex with her. Think of her saying, "No. Busy. Studying." [15-second pause]

You met her the next day, and you are wanting to have sex with her. This time she says, "Yes." [15-second pause]

Think of yourself going to work on Monday. [15-second pause]

Think of yourself going to work a week from now. [15-second pause]

Wanting to have sex with her a week from now, her saying "No." [15-second pause]

Think of the next day. You're wanting to have sex with her and she says, "Yes." [15-second pause]

Think about going to work the next day. [15-second pause]

How does that feel now?

Don: It used to be painful when I would think about it. It doesn't even feel like a missed opportunity, like how I used to think of it—"Aw, I'm missing out." It doesn't feel like that anymore. [Laughter]

It's when she rejects me, then we'll really know.

Don: Overwhelm After FSIP Sex Addiction Session

This session also focuses on avoidance issues.

The following session occurred several weeks after processing Don's compulsions toward massage parlors and pornography. Behaviors are often the result of both a feeling-state and avoidance of feelings. The feeling-states of both behaviors have been processed. In this session, it becomes apparent that Don's recent urges toward those behaviors are the result of avoiding the feeling of being overwhelmed. Therefore, the feeling of being overwhelmed was the focus of treatment for this session.

Don: I went on vacation. Me and my son went on vacation. We came back. When you're coming back from vacation, there was a lot of anxiety because I took the day off work. I had to return the car that we borrowed. I borrowed my mom's car, so I had to return that. I had to do some other stuff. It's like getting back had a lot of anxiety to it because I had to drive like 12 hours to get back in time for his first day in school.

There was a lot of anxiety, and that's when I noticed anxiety has a lot to do with it, too, because I felt like acting out. I felt real anxious. I had stress. I had stuff to do and had that feeling of, "I don't want to do any of it." All I wanted to do was go to a massage parlor or go look at pornography and, kind of, hide away.

Dr. Miller: How long did that last?

Don: It lasted probably a couple hours, until I got everything done. Then, once I got everything done, I, kind of, calmed down. I called my sponsor, and I called some other people in my program and talked it out with them. That's the number one thing I've noticed now is anxiety.

I quit smoking pot. I'm on the second week of that, of not smoking marijuana. That's been tough too. I've also quit cigarettes. I'm going through a lot of stress. That's where I'm having this feeling of acting out because I'm not doing—the only thing I'm doing is drinking beer, maybe a beer a night.

That's about it. I feel a lot of stress from not being able to escape how I used to escape.

Dr. Miller: Let's work on that. Because it sounds like it's no longer about the desire anymore. It's about escaping. What you want to avoid is mainly anxiety?

Don: Yeah, mainly anxiety and the feeling when I get stressed. I want to be able to deal with the stress and not feel like I have to run away from it.

Dr. Miller: What's an example of stress?

Don: This is going to sound weird, but having four or five things to do on my day off. It's my day off. I don't want to do that. I want to sit at home and hang out, or I want to go golfing or something.

Dr. Miller: Are you feeling kind of overwhelmed?

Don: Yeah. That's a good way to put it.

Dr. Miller: Let me tell you what's happening here. When someone feels overwhelmed, you've got four or five things to do, you've got 1,000 things to do, it doesn't make a difference. You feel overwhelmed and stressed because of what you're telling yourself about yourself.

It's not because you have things to do. If I gave you 1,000 things to do in 24 hours, you don't have to feel overwhelmed. You might go, "You're crazy. Can't get it done," or, "Okay, this is what we're going to do and this is how we're going to do this." You'd be task oriented. When you're feeling overwhelmed, it's because of what you're saying about yourself when you're not getting the task done.

You're saying to yourself something like, "I can't do it. It's too much."

Don: "I'll never be able to get it done."

Dr. Miller: "I'll never be able to get it done." If you don't get it done, what does that mean? What's going to happen?

Don: If I don't get it done, then my wife might get mad at me or I'll have to hear it from her.

Dr. Miller: Right. But what does it mean about you?

Don: That I failed.

Dr. Miller: You failed. If you fail, what does that mean about you?

Don: That I'm not good.

Dr. Miller: You're not good. You're a failure.

Don: Exactly.

Dr. Miller: That's why you feel overwhelmed. Not because of having to do a lot of things, but because of what you're telling yourself about what you have to do. So let's change that.

Give me a nightmare image of what's going to happen if you're a failure. What's it going to look like? What's it going to look like for you? I mean, really extreme.

Don: Extreme?

Dr. Miller: Extreme. I want all the elements.

Don: If don't get a project done at work, I'd lose my job. If Susan has given me a "to do" list and I don't get any of it done, she's pissed off at me.

Dr. Miller: What's going to happen? What happens as a result? What's a nightmare result?

Don: What's a nightmare result? I'd have to say that me losing my job—that would be a nightmare result because I wouldn't be able to support my family.

Dr. Miller: What happens to your family? Nightmare.

Don: Nightmare? They would leave.

Dr. Miller: They would leave, okay. You're being abandoned?

Don: Yeah.

Dr. Miller: Nightmare; right?

Don: That's a nightmare.

Dr. Miller: Is that painful or terrifying?

Don: Terrifying.

ImTT Press, publisher

Dr. Miller: Terrifying. What color is the terror?

Don: It's like yellow.

Dr. Miller: Yellow? Where's it located in the body?

Don: Right here (indicating). I feel it. I feel that terror, and it's like I can feel that heartbeat, and I get that flutter.

Dr. Miller: Now see the yellow as being composed of tiny, tiny, tiny little particles of yellow.

Don: Okay.

Dr. Miller: Breathe into the yellow particles. Breathe the yellow particles away from your body.

Don releases the yellow particles of terror with the P/TRP.

Dr. Miller: When you think of that nightmare scenario, how does it seem to you now?

[Pause]

Don: It doesn't seem all that scary. It doesn't even seem like it's possible. When I think about it—really rationally think about it—I think my wife probably won't leave me if I don't get stuff done. If I don't get it done, she's probably not going to leave me. She hasn't left me yet [laughs], and I'm a sex addict.

Dr. Miller: [Laughs]

Don: I think that, as long as I remember that it's not that—

Dr. Miller: It's not about remembering it. How does it seem to you now when you think about it?

Don: When I think about it now, it seems a lot more rational thought that she's not going to leave if I lose my job or if I don't get something done that she wants done.

Dr. Miller: You're not terrified anymore?

Don: No. Not terrified, no.

Dr. Miller: Good. Now, what I want you to do is see that image again. See it composed of tiny little pixel-particles.

[Pause]

Dr. Miller: Now deconstruct the image. Let me know when you're finished.

Don: [Nods]

Dr. Miller: Re-image it again. See if there's a difference between this time and last time.

[Pause]

Don: I think there's a difference because I am picturing myself losing my job and me coming along with my tools in my hand, and I picture her being upset, but I don't picture her stressed out, irate. It's more like, "It will be okay"—upset, but she's, kind of, telling me, "It will be okay."

Dr. Miller: Now pixelate it. Let me know when you've got it.

Don: [Nods]

Dr. Miller: Re-image it again. Tell me what you've got.

Don: The difference is, I have a sense that—when I'm re-picturing it again, that she's not upset but she's more surprised that I lost my job—than anything else—like a shock, an initial shock when I told her that I lost my job. But I still feel like she's more accepting of me. It's not like "I can't believe you lost your job."

It's more of a "We'll get through this together" feeling that I'm feeling.

I guess maybe that's a togetherness feeling, like we're in a marriage and we're a team. We're having a feeling like, "We'll handle it together." It kind of makes me feel good because that's where eventually I'd like to get back to with her. Slowly but surely, we're getting back there.

When I picture myself, I can feel her feelings and then my feelings—they're still kind of scared. I still feel kind of scared. If I'm telling her I'm losing my job, when I re-picture it, that it's more of "What am I going to do?" scared sort of thing.

Dr. Miller: We're going to go through this again. I want you to breathe into the center of your brain and see the pixel-particles go right out the center of your forehead.

Don releases from his body the pixel-particles of the image.

Dr. Miller: When you think of that image, what's your reaction now?

Don: The fear of telling her that I lost my job doesn't seem so overwhelming. I don't feel like I let her down as much, either. Because I think that a lot of it would come—when I'm breathing—I'm doing the breathing and all that. I had this thought come up. I think we might have gone over this—but it's not like the anxiety that's getting me. It's the fear of abandonment that's getting me.

I don't really feel like she's going to leave me anymore, and I don't feel scared to tell her bad news—to tell her that I lost my job, or to tell her that "I couldn't get—the stuff you wanted me to get done, I couldn't get it done."

Dr. Miller: How does it feel now, the idea—like on your day off, you've got four or five things to do. How does that feel now?

Don: I don't feel overwhelmed. It feels like I can do it. If I don't get it all done, the world's not going to end. I'm not going to be letting anybody down if I don't get it done. I also feel that, even if she is mad at me that I didn't get it done, it's not the end of the world.

Even if she is mad at me—which she might be—she might not be, but it's not going to affect me the way I think it's going to affect me. She's not going to get mad and tell me to get out of the house or leave.

Dr. Miller: Which is your nightmare scenario.

Don: Yeah. She's probably like, "I wish you would have got that done."

"Sorry," you know.

Dr. Miller: [Laughs] Now, let's do one more thing. What I want you to do is think of yourself. I want you to focus for about 15, 20 seconds on each thing that I tell you. Don't think of doing it, think about it. Just focus on that particular area. Think of yourself an hour from now.

[Pause]

Dr. Miller: Think of yourself with your wife.

[Pause]

         ImTT Press, publisher

Dr. Miller: Think of yourself going to bed tonight.

[Pause]

Dr. Miller: Think of yourself waking up tomorrow morning.

[Pause]

Dr. Miller: Think of yourself at work.

[Pause]

Dr. Miller: Think of yourself coming home at night.

[Pause]

Dr. Miller: Think of yourself a week from now with your wife.

[Pause]

Dr. Miller: Think of yourself a month from now with your wife.

[Pause]

Dr. Miller: Think of yourself a month from now, at work.

[Pause]

Dr. Miller: Think of yourself six months from now with your wife.

[Pause]

Dr. Miller: Think of yourself six months from now at work. How does that feel? How do you feel?

Don: The main thing, throughout the whole thing, was hopeful. I feel hopeful about my marriage. I feel hopeful about work because, in a month, I'll be starting working somewhere else, so I'm, kind of, hopeful about that.

That's the main thing. I'm hopeful that my marriage is going to get better. I'm hopeful that I will be sober. I'm hopeful for the future, not all doom and gloom.

Dr. Miller: Good. Did you feel pretty much like doom and gloom before?

Don: Yeah. There was a lot of not knowing and feeling scared, like, "I don't know what's going to happen." She might decide it's not working out, or this new job might not work out.

Dr. Miller: Now you're feeling hopeful?

Don: Yeah. It feels like, no matter what happens, I'm still going to be all right. There's plenty of other jobs out there for me to get. I know that my wife wants to work this out. Otherwise, she wouldn't be there. I feel hopeful that things are going to work out, as long as I'm sober. That's the key.

Dr. Miller: Good. Let's review how we've done before, though. In terms of what we've done before, how's that been going?

Don: In terms of what we've done before, it's been going better. I feel like—it's crazy because I don't really think about it. Me and my wife have been getting along pretty well. When we have had arguments, my first reaction wasn't to go act out or to go look at porn. My first reaction was to resolve it, which was nice.

Dr. Miller: That's a good sign.

Don: When you asked me—I'm thinking about it now—we've been getting along really well.

Rusty: Voyeurism—Session #1

Rusty is a 35-year-old married professional who presents for therapy because he was convicted of voyeurism. While he has been controlling his behavior, his voyeuristic urges are intense. In this session, the FSIP is performed on the voyeurism. Fantasy is used to enhance the feeling and make the FS easier to identify.

Dr. Miller: Hello, Rusty.

Rusty: Hello. Just a little background, I had older stepsisters. There were four of them that moved in when I was about five years old. Pretty early on, they began to invite me into their bedroom, and I would lie with them.

They would ask me to give them massages. Then, a lot of times, they would be taking baths so—I would be on the other side of curtain, so it began this—

Dr. Miller: Would you want to peek?

Rusty: I did. Yeah. It was a lot of excitement at the prospect.

Being young, I didn't really know the feelings. I wasn't able to identify them as sexual desire. I liked the feeling that I got when they asked me to spend the night with them or be on the other side of the curtain. So it began.

Dr. Miller: Right. What was on the "other side"? Tell me more about this setup. What do you mean by "the other side of the curtain?"

Rusty: Taking a bath. They were naked. It was like my mind would think, "What do they look like? What are they doing? I know what I do when I bathe. Why were they inviting me in there? Is it something maybe they're wanting me to do but I didn't have the courage to go forward?"

Dr. Miller: When you say the "curtain," you mean the shower curtain?

Rusty: Yes. The shower curtain in the bathtub.

Dr. Miller: And you were on the outside of that curtain?

Rusty: Correct. Yep.

Dr. Miller: Okay.

Rusty: Yeah. It triggered—I think I began to be a voyeur, with some friends around my neighborhood, started spying on them—which ended up being something later on in life that I continued to do. Sometimes, just by circumstance, I would see somebody, maybe, that lived across from me or—searching it out.

ImTT Press, publisher

Dr. Miller: It seems like what happened, when you're on the other side of curtain at that age—is that you wanted to see; right? It's that intense curiosity. "What's going on?" Right? Excitement.

Rusty: Right. Well, I think the feeling was that I was looking into intimacy, like somebody's personal habits. I was, like, a part of that. Even if I was an observer, I got an opportunity to experience that intimacy or that personal connection.

I think my first time, when I saw one of my stepsisters nude, it raised this excitement in me of being a part of what I always wanted to be part of when I'd be behind the curtain or lying next to them and they would ask me to massage them or whatever. I think it was making the connection of "Oh, this is what I was looking for." I think part of that was putting those two pieces together.

I can say that the pornography has increased since I've become married. I never lived with a girl. Most of my dating relationships were pretty fast and quickly over.

I got bored very easily. Now that I've been married to my wife for seven years, I think I haven't dealt well with the long-term connection with her—he intimacy, the commitment.

Dr. Miller: Right. The thing is, once you find it, whatever "it" is, you have to move on because now you've already found it and you have to do it all over again.

That's why marriage gets boring. What I want you to do is think of yourself—imagine yourself on the other side of the curtain. I want you to enhance it. What would make it even more intense?

Rusty: Maybe the curtain wasn't—maybe it would be a little more clear—that I could see a little bit more. I think just a full pull-back would end the excitement. Maybe a frost curtain or something that would allow my mind to, kind of, put pieces together on its own without having it just out there.

Dr. Miller: Okay.

Rusty: Maybe a little bit of the curtain open. I think that's about the best way I can describe it. Having a more frosted curtain versus just a complete dark…

Dr. Miller: What I want you to do is see that image just as you described it, with a kind of translucent curtain. I want you to really let yourself feel that you're almost there. Your mind's almost putting it together. You've got it?

Rusty: Yeah.

Dr. Miller: You can close your eyes if you want to. I need you to really get into it. Just really feel that you're almost there and you're almost about to make this discovery. Feel that almost-eureka moment? that joy moment? that you're about to make a discovery. Okay?

Rusty: Okay.

Dr. Miller: Now I want you to see this image as being composed of tiny little particles, like pixels on a TV screen. Let me know when you've got it.

Rusty: Okay.

Dr. Miller: Now deconstruct the image. You can let the particles fall to the ground or break the image with a sledgehammer, whatever works.

Rusty: Okay.

Dr. Miller: Re-image it again that whole same thing and again tell me what you've got. Is it as intense as it was or does it start to get blurry? What's happening?

Rusty: That's a little harder for me to compose.

Dr. Miller: See it composed of the tiny pixel-particles again. Tell me when you've got it.

Rusty: Okay.

Dr. Miller: Now deconstruct the image. Let me know when you're finished.

Rusty: Okay.

Dr. Miller: Re-image it again and tell me what you've got.

Rusty: Nothing.

Dr. Miller: When you think of being on the other side of that curtain, how does that feel to you now?

Rusty: Neutral.

Dr. Miller: We're now going to do the breathing/visualization protocol for the rest of your body. What I want you to do is visualize that you're breathing into the center of your brain, and breathing those pixel-particles out of your forehead.

Rusty releases from the body the pixel-particles of the image.

Dr. Miller: How do you feel?

Rusty: Clear. If I pull back the curtain, how can I describe it? I'm safer, I guess.

Dr. Miller: So now, when you think of going online and typing in those key words, how does that feel to you now?

Rusty: I guess I don't. I don't really feel the desire or want to—it doesn't seem to have the same feeling. But, normally, when I think about it, my heart races a little bit or even a feeling of guilt or shame. It's so hard to describe.

[Laughter]

Rusty: That's going to be hard to tell you how it feels right now.

Dr. Miller: Nothing's there, huh?

Rusty: Yeah.

Dr. Miller: Okay. This is going to change. This has been a very huge part of your life for a long time. You understand the feeling you're trying to get now?

Rusty: Yeah, I do.

Dr. Miller: You were looking for that joy of discovery and you had connected it to discovering woman's bodies. It was like an adrenaline rush. Everybody wants the joy of discovery.

You just got hooked in with viewing women's bodies. It has to be that initial discovery. That's why typing in the words and everything is so—a big deal with— the sex part of it is not a big deal.

You never really actually had a sex addiction. It was never about the sex.

Rusty: That's good to know.

Dr. Miller: I've actually never seen a sex addiction. It's always the feeling. It's intimacy, it's belonging. I must admit this is the first time that the joy of discovery has been the feeling, but it's never about the sex.

                                       ImTT Press, publisher

There's a positive feeling that links with the behavior. Whether the behavior is watching porn, shopping, gambling or whether it's alcohol or drugs, it's all the same thing. It's all about a positive feeling linked with the behavior. It's the feeling you're looking for and not the behavior. Once you break the link between the feeling and behavior, you're just not interested in doing the behavior anymore.

You have this very intense, powerful feeling that is the "joy of discovery." The feeling of what it means to discover something and the joy of that just got linked up when you were 8 years old. You've been living it out ever since because it was so intense.

The way she tantalized you is why it happened. Your feeling of wanting to discover is a natural, healthy thing that all children should be having. It's just that she seduced you into linking the feeling with looking at females. That's what you've been living out ever since.

Rusty: Lines up with the way I feel.

Dr. Miller: What you are going to notice now is that this has been such a huge part of your life that you may feel pretty disoriented for the next few days and feel strange to yourself because this has been such a large part of your life. You've developed a lot of psychological patterns, including those related to your marriage.

This "joy of discovery" feeling-state has pretty much dominated all your relationships with women. That feeling-state has blocked you from actually going on and discovering a good, intimate relationship because what you've focused on was that tantalizing initial surge of wanting to experience that "joy of discovery."

And then, of course, once you discover whatever it is, you have to do it all over again and again with somebody else. Because it's always got to be somebody new because you've already discovered it and it's no longer that "joy of discovery" anymore. Now the psychological patterns you've developed with your wife are going to change because they are based on the old feelings; and so new behaviors will begin to emerge over time.

You may feel very strange to yourself for a while because you just don't have that old impulse anymore.

Rusty: I look forward to that. [Chuckles]

Dr. Miller: Okay. I don't know if this is the only feeling that's connected to the voyeurism. What I don't know is if there is an additional feeling-state there.

What we just did probably was the most powerful one. Think of it in terms of bright lights. The very, very brightest light hides smaller lights. You can't tell if they are even there. So when the bright light goes out, the lesser lights can be seen.

That's, kind of, what it's like with feeling-states. We very likely eliminated the biggest one, the most important one, but there could be another one in there. We don't know yet.

There is no way to know until you leave and see what goes on for a few days. What we just did, I think, is permanently gone. My point here is that more urges to see women's bodies may surface maybe a week from now—maybe two weeks from now.

Usually, by that time, any other feeling-states that exist are going to surface. But what you may find is that the intense feeling is focused on a different part of that behavior—of the overall behavior. Does that make sense?

Rusty: Yeah.

117

Dr. Miller: For example, if there was something about anal sex that also had a feeling-state connected to that, then that behavior might show up next.

You just have to go through them one at a time until you are finished. What you will notice is that your behavior changes and that the urges will be a lot less than they have been and that your focus of attention will be different.

We can't know if it's all done until some time has passed so that we can see what surfaces. My guess is that this particular behavior is gone.

There may not be anything actually underneath this one, but there might be. I don't know. We'll see what happens.

Rusty: Okay.

ImTT Press, publisher

Rusty: Voyeurism—Session #2

Dr. Miller: How are you doing?

Rusty: I'm actually doing pretty well, I'd say. Better than I've probably done in a long time. I had a fall—about a week ago. That was the first time that I actually pursued or even felt tempted to do anything. I had stepped down to the front to let my dog out. I looked up, and there was a woman, naked in my view, and I was very caught off guard by it. I think had I maybe said something to somebody or talked about it in the moment, I probably would have been able to dispel the power of it—

Dr. Miller: What happened was perhaps another feeling-state got triggered, that's all. It's really unusual to actually process a sexual addiction in one session. People go, they come back, test it out—what's going on—and then we find out what's going on.

You saw a naked woman there. That would be pretty intense. [Laughs] Like "Wow, okay." It's like "Huh?"

So what happened after that?

Rusty: I went to work—that was a Wednesday. I didn't do anything, but it, kind of, stuck in my mind. The next morning it was like I just woke up looking for that very thing. I let my dog out again to try to get a view—seeing what I saw the day before without any effort. I think, after that, I realized, "Uh-oh, I think I'm going down a bad path here." I kept it to myself.

That Thursday night I actually processed it, shared it with some guys that I hang out with on Thursday nights and was able to talk about it. Since then, I haven't even gone out front. I'm just going to stay away from that for now. Friday I fell into pornography, so that was—

Dr. Miller: Tell me what the pornography was.

Rusty: It was on YouTube, just user channels that I have memorized and can go to immediately without needing to search words or anything. It's just—

Dr. Miller: What I mean is what was the pornography? What were the details? What's happening in the pornography? What are you looking at?

Rusty: Just girl-guy sex. I'm trying to think of what I actually looked at because it was— it's never like a catalog, like if you were to go to an actual porn website you could just search what you want, what your preference is, your fetish or whatever. This is different though; it's whatever somebody has uploaded.

I believe what I had looked at is an actual professionally made porn. That was—I think, lasted for about 20 or 30 seconds or so, and I shut it off. I didn't masturbate or anything. I just walked away from it, and I ended up talking to my wife about it that night.

Dr. Miller: When you said, "professionally made," it—

Rusty: A porno. Not an amateur, not a home video or anything.

                                       ImTT Press, publisher

Dr. Miller: For 20, 30 seconds—that's tiny. Is that it? That was the extent of your pornography looking?

Rusty: Yeah. I traced it back to the—what I saw on Wednesday. And since then, mentally, I've traced back to stuff that I did when I was a child with my stepsisters.

Dr. Miller: What else did you do?

Rusty: Had it been just that brief moment, I think I probably would have let it go, but because I took the time to process and see if there was more from this—was I being bothered by something from my past—I felt like, yes, I needed to at least figure out what it meant.

Dr. Miller: When you think about your stepsisters, what's the most positive experience again? Give me the most positive experience, the memories that you were thinking.

Rusty: I really don't have any positive stories; they didn't teach me anything. I'm trying to think of a trip or something that we would have taken together. I was the youngest; so they—

Dr. Miller: Right. But the last time, we processed the bathroom experience; right?

Rusty: Yeah.

Dr. Miller: So I would be looking for something like that again.

Rusty: Not positive versus negative. Like a feeling like I'm—like something—

Dr. Miller: A positive feeling. That was a positive feeling, the joy of discovery. That's pretty powerful.

Rusty: I had a friend over, and the girls were getting ready in the bathroom. We went around to the outside, and they had the bathroom window open; so we had an advantage to be able to watch them get ready. That right there is a pretty powerful moment for me, definitely. It was something that I then continued to pursue with them later a few times.

Dr. Miller: That's a totally different feeling-state right there.

Rusty: What makes this a totally different feeling-state from the shower curtain event?

Dr. Miller: A feeling-state is an isolated memory. We processed the other one, the shower curtain, last time, and that's probably gone. Even if you're getting exactly the same feeling with a slightly different memory of it, it's a different feeling-state because it is a separate, isolated, fixated memory. That's what makes them separate feeling-states.

Rusty: But I have hundreds of memories.

Dr. Miller: Yeah, but they're not all feeling-states. You could have been outside that curtain 50 times and have only one feeling-state about it because it's the same feeling-state being acted out.

You could also have a different feeling connected at the same time. In other words, it could be you feel special because you're outside the curtain and that they're letting you be in the bathroom. It could be any feeling.

What makes it a separate feeling-state is that there is a separate fixation of memory. You could have more than one feeling-state associated with being in the bathroom, but it wouldn't be the same thing. That doesn't mean every time you are in the bathroom with them taking a bath that it formed a feeling-state. Because I am sure it didn't.

ImTT Press, publisher

You might have 50 events and two feeling-states or three feeling-states. But what you're telling me now is there's another experience—that you were with a buddy and you went and saw them. That's a totally different feeling-state now—still a bathroom event—but very, very different. For one thing, there is somebody with you.

The whole thing is very different from what we did last time. As I said, it's not surprising that there is another feeling-state there. That's the norm. That's what usually happens. To have a compulsion going on for a long time in a person's life and have only one feeling-state in regards to that behavior is unusual.

That's why, after the last session, you go and live your life and then see what happens. It's not about fighting the feelings. You got triggered with this naked woman in the window, and there it is. It triggered another feeling-state.

Rusty: Yeah. [Laughs]

Dr. Miller: Let's talk about that experience of being with that guy and looking at your stepsisters. What's the positive feeling? Did they know you were there?

Rusty: No, not at all. The thing I was thinking about was that part—that I was in control. You know, I took the action. I got the bucket so that we could actually see a little bit higher or at a different vantage point. I invited him.

It was different from the "behind the curtain" event because I had no control of the curtain and my stepsister being behind it. I was a passive participant, I guess. This time I was more of an aggressor in the role.

They dominated me a lot, and they beat me up a lot. They chose to separate me from parts of their lives; and I think that was my opportunity to, sort of, have some control and be more aggressive, I guess—if that could be aggressive.

Dr. Miller: So it's a totally different experience.

Rusty: Yeah.

Dr. Miller: When you think back to the whole event—inviting the friend, getting the bucket, standing on the bucket, looking at them—did you see them nude in the bathroom?

Rusty: No. Well, when I first, kind of, took the leap of moving into view, one of my stepsisters—not the one that I normally would be with in the bathroom with the curtain and stuff—the next oldest one. She was just sitting down to use the restroom, and I basically saw her from below the waist down.

That was it, pretty much. She had changed and showered. So I just saw her getting ready from that point on. That first glance was what I saw—I basically saw her bottom half nude.

Dr. Miller: When you think back and imagine running the video of that entire event, where is the most emotional intensity?

Rusty: That first shot—that first glance when I looked in there and saw her. That was the first time I had ever seen that in my life, and so it was this pretty penetrating shot into my heart—like, "Wow, this changes things."

It was very impactful, I think, for me because I saw something that was very new and exciting; but I think part of me knew I shouldn't have been there.

Dr. Miller: It made it more intense.

Rusty: Yeah, yeah.

Dr. Miller: What's the positive feeling?

Rusty: I think my first instinct was to say—was the moment of discovery. There was something I was discovering. Then I think what would be more powerful would be that moment of feeling like I, kind of, got one on top of them. Finally, I'm not—

Dr. Miller: You've got them. You finally got them.

Rusty: Yeah.

Dr. Miller: That made you feel powerful? strong?

Rusty: Yeah.

Dr. Miller: What word would you use?

Rusty: "Victorious," I would—probably would say.

Dr. Miller: Awesome. That's what the feeling-state is. The feeling of victorious linked with the behavior of looking at a woman who doesn't know you are looking at her.

Rusty: Yeah.

Dr. Miller: Let's enhance that image. What makes that image even more powerful? What makes the victory even more so?

Rusty: I guess I'll probably process this out loud. I think, maybe, if I was able to go back and be able to, like, throw it in their face somehow, maybe, or kind of—

Dr. Miller: "I win"? Is it kind of like, "See, I got you"?

Rusty: Yeah.

Dr. Miller: All right. What I want you to do, then, is combine that you're seeing her through the window—you are seeing her genitals—and the feeling is "I got you; see, I got you."

The feeling of how powerful you'd feel after all the time they made you feel weak, that this time you got them; right?

Rusty: Yeah.

Dr. Miller: Got that image?

Rusty: Yeah.

Dr. Miller: Turn it into tiny little pixel-particles.

[Pause]

Rusty: Okay.

Dr. Miller: Now deconstruct the image.

Rusty: Okay.

Dr. Miller: Re-image it again, and tell me what you've got.

[Pause]

Rusty: Definitely less clarity, and I guess I feel a little more calm about it overall. I think, as I was dropping it to the ground, I can feel a sigh of release. It's more jumbled. It's kind of hard for me to put that powerful image back together.

Dr. Miller: Whatever you've got, compose it into tiny particles. Nod your head when you get it.

[Pause. Rusty nods his head]

ImTT Press, publisher

Dr. Miller: Now deconstruct the image

[Pause.   Rusty nods]

Dr. Miller: Re-image it again and tell me what you've got.

Rusty: I was dropping it to the ground. I could feel, kind of, a sigh of release. It's more jumbled. It's hard for me to pick—

Dr. Miller: Re-image it again, and tell me what you've got.

[Pause]

Rusty: There's nothing left.

Rusty releases from the body the pixel-particles of the image.

Dr. Miller: Are you okay?

Rusty: Better than I've probably been in a long time.

Dr. Miller: Okay. How do you feel?

Rusty: I guess, if I try to think about that image, it's moved into all my memories or index cards. This one would have probably had some type of tab on it. I'm able to not see it or pull it out as easy or even think about it. It does not really have the power the way it did when I first brought it up to you today.

I definitely feel like it has been cataloged more properly as a memory among many memories instead of the memory that defines me.

Dr. Miller: Okay. The reason you felt an intense feeling of being victorious is because you had felt just the opposite with them. Remember, you said you felt dominated by them?

Rusty: Yeah.

Dr. Miller: What's the negative feeling that made you want to feel victorious?

Rusty: That somehow I was unworthy of being loved, that somehow—

Dr. Miller: Basically would you say that you felt like you were a loser?

Rusty: Yeah.

Dr. Miller: Basically, with them, you felt like you lost. They won; you lost. Right?

Rusty: Yeah.

Dr. Miller: What I want you to do is give me the image that you lost. Give me an image of that. It could be a memory, a compilation of memories, fantasy included in it—whatever. Give me an image of what it means that you lost.

Rusty: In this context with my stepsisters would be, I think, when I first realized that things had changed at my house. They told me to do their chores, and I stood up to them and I said no. One of the older ones told one of the younger ones to, basically, put me in line and beat me up. So I think that was my first moment of feeling like the dynamic had changed in my house.

Dr. Miller: Okay. So you really lost? You lost the fight?

Rusty: Yeah, at that point. And nobody stood up for me. That's what was—

Dr. Miller: So you really lost?

Rusty: Yeah.

Dr. Miller: Losing is a really big deal. It's very primal, the idea that you lost. So what I want you to do is deconstruct that image. Okay?

Rusty: Okay.

Dr. Miller: When you think of that image, where you realized things had changed and you got beat up. Focus on the point in that whole memory that it hit you that you really lost.

Rusty: That I ended up underneath my bed, crying.

Dr. Miller: Okay. Now, is that image painful or fearful?

Rusty: It's painful.

Dr. Miller: What color is the pain?

Rusty: Red.

Dr. Miller: Where do you see it located in your body?

Rusty: My heart.

Dr. Miller: See that red in your heart as composed of tiny, tiny, little particles. Breathe into those tiny, little red particles and breathe them directly away from your body.

Rusty releases the red particles of pain using the P/TRP.

Dr. Miller: When you think of that event now, does it feel as charged as it was before?

Rusty: No.

Dr. Miller: Good. Now let's finish the deconstruction of it. Do you see the image that you have there? See it composed of tiny, little particles. Let me know when you've got the visualization.

Rusty: [Nods]

Dr. Miller: Now deconstruct the image. Tell me when you're finished.

Rusty: [Nods]

Dr. Miller: Re-image it, and tell me what you've got.

Rusty: Less powerful, definitely. Probably I wouldn't even put "powerful" in it—just another image.

Dr. Miller: Okay. See it composed of tiny little pixel-particles.

Rusty: [Nods]

Dr. Miller: Now deconstruct the image. Tell me when you're finished.

Rusty: [Nods]

Dr. Miller: Re-image it again, and tell me what you have got.

Rusty: Nothing.

Dr. Miller: Okay. All right. Let's go through the body and release the pixel-particles of the image.

Rusty releases from the body the pixel-particles of the image.

Dr. Miller: How do you feel?

Rusty: I feel good, calm.

ImTT Press, publisher

Dr. Miller: When you think of that event that triggered things, how does that feel to you now?

Rusty: I feel fine about it as far as—I don't get excited. I feel I can move on and that it's gone.

Dr. Miller: Okay, good.

Rusty: I knew there was more to the process. It was just—for this just to come across my view—I guess it was just the timing.

Dr. Miller: It's actually good timing. We're not trying for you to be abstinent, which means controlling yourself. The whole advantage of triggering events is that they tell us what there is to process. And we're not just processing the feeling-state.

One of the things we processed today was your belief that you lost and the pain of the loss. That actually has ramifications in all kinds of areas of your life. So the compulsions are just a leading edge of a whole psychological dynamic. When you clear it all the way back from the beginning, all kinds of things change in your life.

We may or may not be totally finished. I don't know. As time goes on, you will find out if there is another feeling-state. If there is, then we will deal with that one.

Rusty: Okay.

ImTT Press, publisher

Rusty: Pornography—Session #3

In the previous two sessions, the focus of treatment has been on Rusty's voyeurism compulsion. Rusty has not had a problem with that behavior since his last session. However, he also has had a problem with watching pornography. At the beginning of the session, Rusty states that he has been worried that the therapy has not been working because he continues to have a problem with pornography. Rusty is actually surprised when he was reminded that we had not worked on that behavior. Rusty's reaction is a good example of the tendency of people to focus on what the current problem is and forget about what no longer bothers them.

Dr. Miller: Hey, Rusty, how you doing?

Rusty: Oh, doing pretty well.

Dr. Miller: What's been happening? It sounds like you were freaking out a little bit there.

Rusty: Yeah, a little bit. I guess it's just hard for me to embrace the process with this., I shouldn't have been surprised, but I was. The incident was—I kind of got this overwhelming sense to search for the first porn that I was exposed to and then start googling some of the images—or some of the events that were taking place in this porn to try to find out what porn it was and then look at it.

I did that, and I figured out what it was, and I watched it. It was definitely hearkening back to my childhood, where I was in this basement with my stepsister and cousins, viewing this porn for the first time.

After that I was trying to think about, "Why all of a sudden did this happen? Why did I have these thoughts? What was I supposed to gain from this—that feeling-state that I was trying to get?"

It was more from when I was younger, when I did this. I believe my boundaries were skewed where my stepsister, the youngest one, Andrea, that I looked at it with. She's also the one that I would be in there in the bathroom with.

At that point, I don't think she was my sister; she was a girl to ogle over or to discover. I don't think the boundaries were ever corrected by my dad or by any family member to say, "She is a stepsister; it's inappropriate."

I never had anybody come in and correct that thinking of "This is wrong; you shouldn't be viewing your sister like this." It created a pattern throughout my life of skewing boundaries of what's appropriate and what's not appropriate in the way I relate to family members.

Dr. Miller: We've never worked on porn.

Rusty: I didn't know that.

Dr. Miller: [Chuckles] We have never worked on porn.

Rusty: [Chuckles] Yeah, you're right. With the voyeurism in the bathroom and then with behind the curtain.

ImTT Press, publisher

Dr. Miller: Then watching them from the outside with your friends.

We've never worked on porn. [Laughter]

Dr. Miller: What's going on in the porn that you're looking at?

Rusty: The first like the old porn that I looked at?

Dr. Miller: Just start off with that. What did you watch with your stepsister?

Rusty: It was '70s porn, vintage kind of thing. It was a woman and a man. Just kind of a lot more plot than nowadays, I guess. [Laughter]

Rusty: It's, kind of, more of a VHS feel to it than a high def. There isn't anything in it that would stand out in my mind. Like, I think it was just a scene that I saw involving a woman and a guy at a dinner table. Beyond that, there wasn't anything that stood out, I guess.

Dr. Miller: Your stepsister invited you to do this?

Rusty: We were watching *Money Can't Buy Me Love*. I don't know if you're familiar with that '80s movie, but we were just watching a movie, and it cut at the end straight right to porn. It was harmless in that we weren't seeking it out. I didn't even know what porn was at that point in my life. When that movie cut, you can tell it was taped over.

It was my stepsister. It was my cousin's dad. My cousin was a couple of years younger than me. My stepsister was a couple of years older than me. We were down there watching a movie in the den, and this porn just, kind of, appeared on the screen.

Dr. Miller: When it appeared, what did you do while watching it?

Rusty: I think I remember being, like, startled by the images—at the same time, very excited. I don't think I got an erection or anything. I was pretty young. I think I was very intrigued by what was happening. I knew in the moment what we were doing was wrong. It's not like we searched it out. It just appeared from that.

Dr. Miller: What was the interaction with your stepsister like?

Rusty: We didn't touch or do anything like that. I think we were both, kind of, shocked and, like, just watched it. I don't even remember watching just a little bit before we got really nervous about it. Somebody could discover us watching it. I think it was more of that. We didn't want it taken away from us. We stopped it and re-winded it and put it back in its place.

We went back to it. I remember wanting to go back to his house to see it over and over and trying to get him to let me go down to his basement and watch it more and wanted to stay overnight. I think his dad eventually figured out that we were watching it and removed them.

Dr. Miller: When you would go over there, were you watching it with your stepsister?

Rusty: It did happen on more than one occasion that I watched it with her. I watched it more than once without her also.

Dr. Miller: Now, it triggered you looking at other porn; is that true?

Rusty: Yeah.

Dr. Miller: You've been looking at porn every day. What is the content of that porn?

Rusty: Within the confines of YouTube, I have certain users that I could go to and figure out if they've got porn on their channel. It's whatever is available. It's not really anything specific. It's mainly heterosexual girl-guy porn.

Dr. Miller: When you're searching it out, what's the most exciting point of that? When you're typing in the words? When you are watching it?

Rusty: Probably not so much watching it. Probably that moment right before I click on watching it, there's a point where I can shut it down. It's like a thumbnail (small picture on the screen). You see it. It's that. You've got one toe in, sort of—like, do you just go ahead and click "play," or do you just shut it down. There's that moment where it's like, "Okay. I'm in."

Dr. Miller: This is another feeling-state of the behind-the-curtain variety. In other words, when you're just about to know what's going on.

Rusty: I was thinking—I'm, like, "Man, if this is just—again, the discovery—is this different, or is it new?"

Dr. Miller: What's happened is that you can have the same feeling connected to different events. For you, discovery was just a really big deal. There's something about your wanting to know. When you're saying that you went back to that old porno, I imagined that the most intense part was when you discovered it again.

Rusty: For sure. I was actually kind of surprised in that I hadn't searched it out before. It wasn't even a thought, but, all of a sudden, it became very intense. Once you watch it, you start remembering the scenes and where I was and who I was with. That first time I watched it again was the most intense. It kind of degraded from there.

Dr. Miller: Because you discovered it. When you watch porn, do you ever re-watch the same thing?

Rusty: No.

Dr. Miller: We're still dealing with the same basic feeling. Let's work on it. The thumbnail—there it is. It's the thumbnail. That's where it's most intense. I want you to really let yourself feel, there it is—"The joy of discovery." Really let yourself feel that joy of discovery. There it is—"The joy of discovery."

What do you think you're about to discover? What's your fantasy about what you're about to discover? What might it be? Make it up—just a fantasy—from when you were a child. What might you discover?

Rusty: That I've been let in on some big secret that has been hidden from me up until that point. I mean that feeling of, kind of, "Ah-hah," like, "Wow!" It was a really big deal for me. I think being able to share that connection—where if I'm alone, I'm discovering it by myself, but it involves getting let in on some—

Dr. Miller: You're part of the group that is let in on the secret?

Rusty: Yeah.

Dr. Miller: What's the word? If you are let in on the secret, you "fit in"? you "belong"? you're "part of the group"?

Rusty: Yeah.

ImTT Press, publisher

Dr. Miller: How would you put it?

Rusty: I've been given a role to play that was previously unknown or not available to me. I've got choice. I've got options. I've got status, but just—like, I'm important. I'm included.

I think I was definitely excluded a lot, being the youngest. And I was constantly trying to be included. I was very much somebody that had to fight to be included in on what my stepsisters or my brothers were doing. I think it was—a moment where I had inclusion on an event—that was very big. It was very major, I think, seeing sex for the first time, not knowing what it was.

Dr. Miller: Now you are included.

Rusty: Now I "know."

Dr. Miller: That feeling that you're "included" is what you keep seeking out by watching the porn. Does this sound right?

Rusty: Yeah. And maybe even the fear of missing out. It's sick, but it's like—yeah.

Dr. Miller: You desperately have always wanted to be included, and the more you see, the more included you are. That's what it feels like.

Rusty: Yeah.

Dr. Miller: Let's work this out. There you are about to be included. This time I don't want this to be that realistic. I want you to do it like with five different pornos and five different thumbnails, and you're going to be included in that group. Give me an image. What does it look like to you? What really hypes it up—that you are included?

Rusty: If I was asked to be included, I think. If there was to be an invitation.

Dr. Miller: What does that look like in the image if you're going to be included? Just your stepsister asking you to be included?

Rusty: Yeah. I think it would be that she would initiate inviting me to go back and look at it with her.

Dr. Miller: Let's use that image. You're feeling she's inviting you to go back and look at it with her. You're feeling very included. See that image composed of tiny little pixel-particles. Just nod your head when you get it.

Rusty: [Nods]

Dr. Miller: Now deconstruct the image. Tell me when you're finished.

Rusty: [Nods]

Dr. Miller: Re-image it again, and tell me what you've got.

Rusty: I've got her standing there and me feeling important, special feeling of warmth, that there's something I've always desperately wanted.

Dr. Miller: Now pixelate the image. Tell me when you're finished.

Rusty: [Nods]

Dr. Miller: Now deconstruct the image. Tell me when you're finished.

Rusty: [Nods]

Dr. Miller: Re-image it again, and tell me what you've got.

Rusty: I'm by myself this time and not feeling anything at all.

ImTT Press, publisher

Dr. Miller: In the image, you're not included in it at all?

Rusty: No.

Rusty releases from his body the pixel-particles of the image.

Dr. Miller: What I want you to do now is to notice the feeling of being not included. Is that painful or terrifying?

Rusty: Painful.

Dr. Miller: What color is the pain?

Rusty: Black.

Dr. Miller: Where is it located?

Rusty: My stomach.

Dr. Miller: See that black as composed of little, tiny particles. Breathe into the tiny black particles, and breathe them directly away from the stomach.

Rusty releases the black particles of pain with the P/TRP.

Dr. Miller: When you think of the image of not being included, does it feel less charged than it was?

Rusty: I don't feel that was the case. I think, once the image broke free, I started seeing a lot of times when I was included. I had friends that—I got picked first in backyard football. I ran around feeling included with other groups of people, but—that wasn't the case. I guess I had locked in on that memory of not being included. It just, kind of, unraveled like a whole lot of themes, with me playing in the woods with friends and a lot of different times where I didn't feel that way.

Dr. Miller: That's the power of images. You had this one image that you were not included, and that's what you lived off of and, in so many ways, that you acted out from. Now let's go back. I want to see, though, is there anything left to that image of you not being included? Did it all just dissolve, or did it become less powerful?

Rusty: I feel like it is significantly, if not altogether, gone.

Dr. Miller: Is it like a ghost of itself or something?

Rusty: What is that?

Dr. Miller: Is it kind of like a ghost of itself?

Rusty: Yeah. A lot of things are moving into the forefront of my mind that, I guess, in some respect, should have had more sway on me than that one image did.

Dr. Miller: Is there anything left of that image? If there is anything left, we need to finish it off.

Rusty: Not that I'm able to, not—yeah.

Dr. Miller: Can you think of going to look at porn? How does that seem to you now?

Rusty: Insignificant. I don't need it. I think, beforehand, I would definitely have said that it has some weightiness to it, that I was able definitely to picture certain thumbnails. Right now it's just like a blank slate.

ImTT Press, publisher

Dr. Miller: Is it beginning to make sense to you what's been going on with you?

Rusty: Especially after, as we were working the particles down and breaking that image. It was like a floodgate had opened up that there was more going on in my life than I let on there was. I think I've picked pieces that were significant and elevated them into my identity, like who I was—insignificant, I wasn't included, I was unloved, unworthy of being loved. Those things did manifest themselves, but that wasn't all me, growing up. I had fun discovering stuff in the woods, and there are tons of things that I've blocked out for a long time because I have been afraid.

My childhood for me has been associated with those events, and the way I related to my stepsisters kept me from going back out of fear of what it would do to me mentally and emotionally. So I can't say I'm not a little afraid, but I definitely don't have the fear that I had before—at least, in this moment.

I'm sitting here going back and just trying to piece some puzzle pieces together because I do want to share some stuff with my daughter. She's very much like me, and I want her to be excited about discovery and not fear what that means, if you know—

Dr. Miller: It's really interesting. Your need for discovery is really large, very intense, and it just got hooked into the wrong things. Sexuality was involved, as well as your feeling excluded. There was a combination. It was a connection between the two that made it very powerful. Your natural personality is to want to discover things.

Rusty: I've had this problem a long time. How can it go away so fast?

Dr. Miller: The length of time you've had a compulsion is not relevant in terms of releasing it. If we had gotten to it six months after it started, it would be gone. If we'd processed it 50 years after it started, it would be gone. The intervening time is irrelevant in terms of processing. It doesn't make any difference; it's the same thing. You're doing the same thing, basically, acting out exactly the same feeling-state again and again and again.

One misconception people have is that they think that, if you've been doing the behavior a long time, then it's really grooved into you—it's a long-standing habit or a long-standing compulsion. Long standing is irrelevant. It doesn't make any difference. You're just doing the same thing again and again and again. It doesn't become more grooved. It doesn't become more of you, other than the way it's part of your whole life.

The feeling-state is just a feeling-state. It doesn't get more powerful. It stays the same. Its power doesn't increase with age. It doesn't decrease with age. It just stays there. Does that make sense?

Rusty: Yeah, a little.

131

Dr. Miller: You've had three different feeling-states. They were created, they exist, and they continue to exist until you deconstruct them. Once you deconstruct them, how long before you actually got to treatment is not relevant. It's just a number, the number of days, months, or years that measure how long it took you to get there.

These are three different images that you have. Take the image that you have about not being included. It was certainly not true, but the image was so powerful. The image was powered—really, energized—by what you needed—to feel included in your family.

Being included with football and with your friends is one thing, but we all want to be included with our family, and that's really intense. Because of the difficulties you had with your family, that image became intensely energized. So that's the image you've been dancing around in your life.

Once it's de-energized, you go, "Oh, wow. There's all these other parts of myself too. I was doing this. I was doing that. I was included here."

Now that you're not blinded by that one image, you can see all the other ways that you did things, when you look back in your childhood.

Rusty: That resonates with how I feel. I guess, once you start breaking those images, it, kind of, gives you a freedom.

Dr. Miller: It does. You can see yourself now. Images keep us from feeling what's inside ourselves, what we really want. You create these images in your childhood, and you just keep acting from them. Some of the images from childhood are less intense and affect your behavior less intensely. But the images still affect the way you think of yourself.

It will take a while, by the way. You'll probably spend months allowing the changes to go through your unconscious and come up with what really works for you.

Rusty: Sweet.

ImTT Press, publisher

Winton: Bondage Fantasy

Winton had an intense sexual bondage fantasy that was focused on a close friend. Even though he is attracted to women, he is concerned that he appears to be sexually attracted to men since the object of his sexual fantasy is male. The fantasy involves sadistic feelings linked with sexual excitement and Winton's desire for his existence to be acknowledged.

Dr. Miller: Tell me what's going on.

Winton: I have same-sex attraction. This is unwanted because I'd like this not to be the case. I've never been intimate with another man, but I do have fantasies. I have a desire for some specific men to share more intimate kinds of things. I feel like this is coming more from an idea of dominating the other person.

I feel insecure that I might lose the other person; so I have a desire for possession that manifests itself, at times, with sexual connotations.

Dr. Miller: When you have a situation like that—you're right—it's not sexual.

Winton: I'm sorry? Again?

Dr. Miller: When you have a situation like that—even though it seems to be about sex, it's really not.

Winton: Oh, okay.

Dr. Miller: As you said, it's really about domination. That's not sex. Okay? It has nothing to do with sexual orientation whatsoever.

Winton: I see. I don't know. I feel—I don't—

Dr. Miller: I'm not saying you don't feel sexually excited when imagining the fantasy.

Winton: Right. That's right.

Dr. Miller: It's really not about sexual orientation.

Winton: I struggle—if I don't feel sexually aroused, I don't understand why this wouldn't be sexual, then—wouldn't relate the fantasy to sex, then.

Dr. Miller: I'll give you an example. I had a person who had a fetish about angora sweaters. The sweater became this thing that really turned him on. He always wanted his wife to wear an angora sweater.

Winton: I see.

Dr. Miller: It had to do with his mother wearing an angora sweater when he was a toddler while she was carrying him around. So the angora sweater became sexualized even though it has no gender whatsoever. Whatever your gender orientation is, this won't change it. In other words, these fantasies don't mean anything in terms of what your orientation is. It's absolutely irrelevant—is probably the best way to say it.

Winton, tell me more about the fantasy.

Winton: I am in my bed, and this colleague friend is also there. He is very excited, and he is restrained so he can't touch himself. I'm the only one who can do it and, if I do it, he gets more excited.

He looks at me. He asks for more. The penetration with objects does happen, is not always present in the fantasy. It doesn't necessarily add much more.

Dr. Miller: How do you penetrate him? Do you have anal sex? What kind of sex?

Winton: No. No, I wouldn't—I don't know. [Laughs] It would be some objects from my hand. I don't know which because I'm very [Laughs] inexperienced on this point of view; so my imagination becomes very vague on this aspect. [Laughs] I just know that I'm—

Dr. Miller: Penetrating him.

Winton: Yes. But I don't know what objects I'm using.

Dr. Miller: Let's not worry about that, then.

Winton: Okay.

Dr. Miller: When you penetrate him, what are you feeling? I know you feel excited, but that's not the feeling we're looking for here. Do you feel complete?

Winton: It feels like some kind of wild anger. Yeah, some kind of sadistic feeling, almost.

Dr. Miller: So you want to hurt him. There's a part of you that wants to hurt him.

Winton: Yeah.

Dr. Miller: When you hurt him, what's the positive feeling of hurting him?

Winton: Even if I hurt him, I don't see him unhappy about it.

Dr. Miller: What's the positive feeling?

You're hurting him. Is it like revenge?

Winton: I feel like now he cannot ignore me. Yeah, some desire of attention that isn't responded to.

Dr. Miller: So he finally has to acknowledge you.

Winton: Right. I guess so.

Dr. Miller: That's when you know you exist. When you penetrate him and you hurt him, it's like you're saying, "You're finally going to notice me."

Winton: Yes. I think that's correct.

Dr. Miller: What I want you to do now is to close your eyes and really notice the fantasy—there you are and you're penetrating him. You're not only feeling the anger and the desire to hurt him, you're also feeling noticed, acknowledged. Just nod your head when you get it, really as intense as you can. Really rip it, right there in the fantasy of it. Enhance it any way you can—that he's screaming more—whatever he's doing.

Winton: Okay.

ImTT Press, publisher

Dr. Miller: Now what I want you to do is pixelate it, like pixels on a TV screen. Pixelate it. See the whole fantasy pixelated.

Winton: Okay.

Dr. Miller: Now deconstruct that whole image in any way you want to.

Winton: Okay.

Dr. Miller: All right. Now re-image it again, and tell me what you've got.

Is it just as strong as it was? Is it beginning to fade? What's happening?

Winton: When I reconstruct it—

Dr. Miller: Reconstruct the whole fantasy all over again.

Winton: The same as before?

Dr. Miller: Same as before. You're penetrating him. You're angry. You're hurting him. He's acknowledging your existence. You're not only being acknowledged—is that beginning to fade? Is it the same intensity as before or what?

Winton: Less intense than before.

Dr. Miller: Pixelate it again.

Winton: Okay.

Dr. Miller: Deconstruct it.

Winton: Okay.

Dr. Miller: All right. Re-image it again. Tell me what you've got.

Winton: It loses in power. I become more sad. I don't know if this is important.

Dr. Miller: That's a natural reaction.

But the image still is there—right?—to some degree?

Winton: Yeah, it is.

Dr. Miller: Pixelate whatever the image is there.

Winton: Okay.

Dr. Miller: Deconstruct it.

Winton: Okay.

Dr. Miller: Re-image it again. Tell me what you've got.

Winton: In terms of seeing or in terms of feeling?

Dr. Miller: How much is the image beginning to fall apart? fade away?

Winton: It's falling apart. My fun is losing its identity. I can't—

Dr. Miller: Whatever is left, pixelate it.

Winton: Okay.

Dr. Miller: Deconstruct it.

Winton: Okay.

Dr. Miller: Re-image it again. Tell me what you've got.

Winton: It has no effect on me anymore. The scene is losing, completely, its details.

Dr. Miller: But it's still present? Pixelate it again.

Winton: [Sighs] Okay.

                                       ImTT Press, publisher

Dr. Miller: Deconstruct it.

Winton: Okay.

Dr. Miller: Re-image it again. Tell me what you've got.

[Pause]

Winton: It's hard to describe. I'm still on the bed. That is still there, but the other person—I can't distinguish a face or other connotations.

Dr. Miller: Pixelate whatever is there.

Winton: Okay.

Dr. Miller: Deconstruct it. Just tell me what you see. Imagine that the pixel-particles are going into the earth. See the pixel-particles just being absorbed, absorbed, absorbed—just going into the earth. Pixel-particles are just draining into the earth. The earth is just taking away all these pixel-particles, draining it, draining it, and draining it.

Winton: Okay.

Dr. Miller: Re-image it again. Tell me what you've got.

Winton: I hope I'm not making this up, but I see the figure has a female connotation now.

Dr. Miller: Is it a positive image? What's going on with the image now?

Winton: It's still naked—this figure—but I'm not doing any action.

Dr. Miller: Tell me, do you have a positive reaction to it?

Winton: Yes.

Dr. Miller: Or is it just neutral?

Winton: No. It's positive. It makes me feel at ease.

Dr. Miller: Let's try one more iteration of this, if it's there. Pixelate it.

Winton: Okay.

Dr. Miller: Deconstruct it. See all the pixel-particles draining to the earth, draining deeply, deeply, deeply—being absorbed, absorbed, absorbed.

Winton: [Sighs] Okay.

Dr. Miller: Re-image it again. Tell me what you've got.

Winton: I'm still on the bed. I am holding the legs. "Holding," meaning putting my hands on top of the legs of this person whom I don't know is—he—she—it. [Pause] Maybe I'm holding some kind of cylindrical objects. [Pause] It's from about the belly button or above the chest that—there is nothing of this person I can identify.

Dr. Miller: Okay. Pixelate the image.

Winton: Okay.

Dr. Miller: Deconstruct it.

[Pause]

Winton: Okay.

Dr. Miller: Re-image it again, and tell me what you've got.

[Pause]

Winton: I noticed that my arms are really small, like I'm a kid.

ImTT Press, publisher

Dr. Miller: Okay.

Winton: I'm losing it. I'm struggling to focus on the image.

Dr. Miller: Okay. Pixelate whatever's there.

Winton: Okay.

Dr. Miller: Deconstruct it.

[Pause]

Winton: Okay.

Dr. Miller: Re-image it again. Tell me what you've got.

[Pause]

Winton: The only details I can now reconstruct is the belly button, this black hole.

Dr. Miller: Pixelate whatever is there, and deconstruct it.

Winton: Okay.

Dr. Miller: See all the pixel-particles go into the ground, go into the earth, and be absorbed, absorbed, absorbed into the earth.

Winton: Okay.

Dr. Miller: All right. Re-image it. Tell me what you've got.

[Pause]

Winton: It's again the belly button.

Dr. Miller: Okay.

Winton: Yeah. I think that's what it is.

Dr. Miller: Is it beginning to fade more? Is it the same as it was?

Winton: No. It's bigger. And it's not—from my experience, I would say it's female. I don't know. There are no ab muscles that would give me the impression it's a man.

Dr. Miller: Pixelate it.

Winton: Okay.

Dr. Miller: Deconstruct it.

[Pause]

Winton: Okay.

Dr. Miller: Re-image it, and tell me what you've got.

Winton: It's just basically a black hole.

Dr. Miller: Look at it.

Winton: I can still see the border as pink, like flesh, but the inside has become much bigger and is just a hole that I can't see the bottom of.

Dr. Miller: Pixelate it.

Winton: Okay.

Dr. Miller: Deconstruct it.

Winton: Okay.

Dr. Miller: Re-image it again. Tell me what you've got.

[Pause]

Winton: It's like a circular hole in the ground, like a well. I don't know.

Dr. Miller: Pixelate it.

Winton: Okay.

Dr. Miller: Deconstruct it.

[Pause]

Winton: Okay.

Dr. Miller: Re-image it again. Tell me what you've got.

[Pause]

Winton: It's more like a well. I guess I'm doing some association. I see a well.

Dr. Miller: Pixelate it.

Winton: Okay.

Dr. Miller: Deconstruct it.

[Pause]

Winton: Okay.

Dr. Miller: Re-image it again. Tell me what you've got.

[Pause]

Winton: Sweet. This is, kind of, the same image. I don't know. It gains some—the color—the pink color, is gone. It's green.

Dr. Miller: Pixelate it.

Winton: Okay.

Dr. Miller: Deconstruct.

Winton: Okay.

Dr. Miller: Re-image it again. Tell me what you've got.

Winton: I don't know whether this makes sense. I gave some geographical location to this well. I don't know. I feel like I'm somewhere—it's a very green mountain.

Dr. Miller: Anyplace you know, or just in your imagination?

Winton: I think it is a mix of other things, but the main structure reminds me of the mountains where I grew up, in Colorado.

Dr. Miller: How does that feel to you?

Winton: It feels peaceful, but I feel alone. I see all the scenery, but I'm on my own.

Dr. Miller: Pixelate it.

Winton: Okay.

Dr. Miller: Deconstruct it.

[Pause]

Winton: Okay.

ImTT Press, publisher

Dr. Miller: Re-image it again. Tell me what you've got.

[Pause]

Winton: I added more details to it. It's like more of a forest around.

Dr. Miller: Pixelate it.

Winton: Okay.

Dr. Miller: Deconstruct.

[Pause]

Winton: Okay.

Dr. Miller: Re-image it again. Tell me what you've got.

[Pause]

Winton: I feel like I'm getting into some memories instead of images. Is that okay, or should I try—

Dr. Miller: What memories are you getting into?

Winton: When I think about the forest and the mountains and where I thought I was, it makes me think of when I was a kid. I used to go to this mountain with my mother, brother, a friend, and his father. It was a really tall mountain.

Dr. Miller: Are they good memories?

Winton: Yeah. I always thought so. Yeah. I thought they were good memories. Yes, I think.

Dr. Miller: What we're going to do now is we're going to go back to the original memory and remove those pixel-particles from your body.

Winton: The original memory or the one I just described?

Dr. Miller. The fantasy of the domination—those are the pixel-particles we need to remove. The good image—the final image is fine. We don't need to deal with that. Okay?

Winton: Okay.

Dr. Miller: Breathe into the center of your brain so that the pixel-particles of the old, original image go out your forehead.

Winton releases from the body the pixel-particles of the image.

Dr. Miller: All right. How do you feel?

[Pause]

Winton: How do I feel? I feel very relaxed.

Dr. Miller: When you think of that fantasy, what's your reaction now?

[Pause]

Winton: The penetration aspect now is more a feeling of disgust that I don't want to do. Indeed, I don't even want to get close to his spot. And the masturbation—on one hand, I don't want to touch his penis because I feel a bit disgusted by that, but I still have the lingering feeling of desiring his approval.

Dr. Miller: Does desiring his approval have any sexual connotations at this time?

Winton: No, it doesn't necessarily. It doesn't. I feel like I just really want it, for some reason.

                                       ImTT Press, publisher

Dr. Miller: Do you understand now what the fantasy was all about?

Winton: I don't understand the connection I had with my memories at all, but I understand that my desire is for his approval, yes.

Dr. Miller: What the fantasy—desire for his approval has nothing whatsoever to do with what we just processed.

Winton: I see.

Dr. Miller: That's just something else. That's more normal.

Winton: I like to hear the word "normal."

Dr. Miller: What your fantasy was really about was getting someone to acknowledge you. You have felt very unacknowledged—like, "Notice me," "Pay attention to me." This is a three- or four-year-old saying, "Pay attention." Children need desperately for their parents to pay attention to them—I don't mean just "look" pay attention—but to acknowledge their existence. You needed your parents to make you feel that you existed in their presence—in the presence of another person.

When your parent looks at you and gazes into your eyes, they're basically saying, "You exist."

Winton: I see.

Dr. Miller: That's what you were looking for in this fantasy. Many, many years ago, you didn't get that kind of deep acknowledgment of your existence. That's what was missing.

Winton: I don't know when that could have happened because I feel like my parents were quite present.

Dr. Miller: You know something? Somewhere along the line, it happened. These fantasies don't just come out of the blue.

You didn't "catch a cold." This wasn't like the flu season, where a bunch of people catch it. It can only come from something in your past.

Winton, is it possible that the "well" memory links to that? Because you went to the well, and you described it as peaceful but lonely. Does that somehow fit with this feeling of being unacknowledged?

Might there be an association—or no? I don't want to read information into it that's not there.

Winton: The feeling is very similar, indeed, but I don't know.

What is that memory? I don't recall any well where this mountain was.

Dr. Miller: You know something? This was not a well. This was an image. This was not a physical well. The well was your transition from one image to another. It was like you were boring a hole from one place to another in your mind.

Winton: Wow, our brain really does that? That's really cool.

ImTT Press, publisher

Dr. Miller: Yes. It's why I kept going after it. It's as if your mind was trying to completely dispel the old image and was moving through a tunnel into a new image.

The new image was the positive one with the mountains and the forest, but somewhere along the line, you had this feeling. You know something? It could've been when you were three or four or five years old and it happened one time and, yet, it was so intense, it fixated.

This doesn't have to be something that was predominantly true. It could be that, somewhere along the line, you really, really desperately needed to be acknowledged and it didn't happen. These things just don't happen out of the blue. It comes out of your experience somewhere.

Winton: I see.

Dr. Miller: Okay?

Winton: But if it is an experience, it cannot be changed.

Dr. Miller: You just changed it.

Winton: Did I? But I—[laughs]—I don't know what happened. How could I have changed it? I don't know what this memory is.

Dr. Miller: It doesn't make any difference. You don't have to know the memory. You have images, and you just changed it. It's not what happened that's important. It's what's in your mind that's important.

The effect of any experience is what's in your mind, and you changed what's in your mind. You can change preverbal experiences, for example, things you do not remember, but if you have an image that resonates with that feeling, with that experience that happened, then you change the effect of what happened.

Winton: I see.

Dr. Miller: Now, something that may happen over the next week is that you may start to feel somewhat disoriented.

Winton: I feel disoriented now.

Dr. Miller: Okay. It's, like, "Who am I?"

This has been a very, very powerful image in your life, and you're going to find a lot of things change.

Winton: I hope so. Wow.

Dr. Miller: You'll notice it most in the next few days. Usually by 10 days, the disorientation is over with. Then you're just going to find sometimes you just don't do what you used to do. This will continue changing for maybe six months or more.

These kinds of secret sexual fantasies are major images in a person's life. Most people don't act them out. They don't act on them, but even though they don't act out on them, the fantasies still take up tremendous amounts of the person's energy, and they do alter a lot of behaviors.

Winton: I think I understand. I've already done this process. I'm surprised. I feel very disoriented, that's true, right now.

Yes, I just remembered something. I don't know.

I hope everything you said is right. It will be amazing.

Dr. Miller: Okay.

ImTT Press, publisher

Transcripts

Utilizing the FSAP and P/TRP

Utilizing the Feeling-State Addiction Protocol and the P/TRP to Heal the Wounds of Loss of a Relationship

---

Ann: Releasing the Pain and Attachment After the Breakup of a Relationship—Session #1

Ann had ended a relationship with a boyfriend a few months before the session. The problem was that she was having difficulty moving on with her life. These two transcripts focus on the following two issues:

1. Releasing the pain caused by the broken relationship, and
2. Breaking the attachment to her ex-boyfriend caused by feeling-states.

Ann: I'm having issues getting over the guy that I just recently ended things with a couple of months ago. I'm still just stuck on him. I still find myself crying at night over it.

Dr. Miller: Then it's very current; we need to deal with that.

Ann: Okay.

Dr. Miller: Let's start off with the pain of it. When you think of him and the breaking up of the relationship, what color is the pain?

Ann: Black.

Dr. Miller: Where do you see it?

Ann: At my heart.

Dr. Miller: Let's release it.

Ann releases the black particles of pain with the P/TRP.

Ann: I don't feel anything or I don't see any more black. That one was harder for me, though, to do.

Dr. Miller: It's very current.

Ann: Yeah.

Dr. Miller: When you think of him, what comes up for you now?

Ann: Everything. Us dancing together. His smiles—his seven different smiles. Oh!

Dr. Miller: The pain is gone, but you're now missing him more; right?

Ann: Yeah.

Dr. Miller: What's the most positive experience you have ever had with him?

Ann: Valentine's Day

Dr. Miller: Tell me about it.

Ann: We had just started dating, and all week we were both kidding about Valentine's Day. He asked me if I wanted to spend Valentine's Day with him.

I said, "Yeah. Nothing special. No big deal." Then I go there, and he surprises me with flowers, cookies, and chocolate. Then he took me out dancing—which was my favorite thing to do and no one ever does it—and he sang to me. It was the funnest night I ever had. It was enjoyable.

Dr. Miller: How did it make you feel?

Ann: It made me feel special.

Dr. Miller: Now what we're going to do is a different protocol.

Ann: Okay.

Dr. Miller: Was there some point when you felt more special than the other time?

Ann: Yeah.

Dr. Miller: Right there? Some point in that day?

Ann: Not at that day; it was a different day.

Dr. Miller: Was that the most special day, though?

Ann: Yeah. That was the most special.

Dr. Miller: Then let's stay with that.

Ann: Okay

Dr. Miller: And just how special did you feel, being with him? On a 0-to-10 scale—where zero means that you don't feel anything and 10 means that you feel absolutely the most special—where would you put it?

Ann: An 8.

Dr. Miller: An 8. Where do you feel it in your body?

Ann: The torso. The whole torso.

Dr. Miller: What I want you to do is to follow this wand.

BLS — Eye Movements

Dr. Miller: Now, when you think of that again, how intense is it? More intense, less intense, or staying the same?

Ann: It's less intense.

Dr. Miller: Focus in on it again.

BLS — Eye Movements

ImTT Press, publisher

Dr. Miller: Does it feel more intense, less intense, or staying the same?

Ann: Just slightly less intense, but much more less intense than the first time.

Dr. Miller: What number would you put now?

Ann: A 5—4-1/2, actually.

Dr. Miller: 4-1/2. All right.

BLS — Eye Movements

Dr. Miller: What's happening for you now? Is it more intense? less intense?

Ann: Definitely less intense.

Dr. Miller: What number would you put it now?

Ann: A 3.

Dr. Miller: Stay with that.

BLS — Eye Movements

Ann: A 2.

Dr. Miller: A 2? Okay

BLS — Eye Movements

Ann: 1.

Dr. Miller: Your mind was wandering a bit that time.

Ann: Yeah.

Dr. Miller: [Laughs]

Ann: One more time.

Dr. Miller: Where are you now?

Ann: I guess at 1/2. It's really nothing, but it's not nothing.

Dr. Miller: Not quite nothing.

Ann: Yeah.

Dr. Miller: All right. Let's try it one more time now.

BLS — Eye Movements

Ann: Nothing.

Dr. Miller: Nothing. Can you feel your general need to feel special?

Ann: Yeah.

Dr. Miller: When you let yourself really feel that, what number would you put it?

Ann: When I let myself really feel that?

Dr. Miller: Really feel the need to feel special.

Ann: What is my scale? 1 to 10?

Dr. Miller: 0 to 10.

Ann: I feel a 10.

Dr. Miller: Where do you feel it in your body?

Ann: My chest. Really, that's where I hold everything, I guess.

BLS — Eye Movements

                                       ImTT Press, publisher

Dr. Miller: What number would you put it now?

Ann: My need for attention? Just, like, overall?

Dr. Miller: To take care of the general need to feel special.

Ann: An 8-1/2.

Dr. Miller: 8-1/2? See, what we're doing is—you have a really intense need to feel special. That's what gets you in trouble. Everybody has a certain healthy need to feel special. This intensity is not healthy. We're just taking away the unhealthy part. Okay?

Ann: Got it.

Dr. Miller: Focusing on it again.

BLS — Eye Movements

Ann: Probably an 8. I'm feeling anxious again.

Dr. Miller: What are you feeling anxious about?

Ann: I don't know. Something's very unhealthy—wrong with me, I guess. I'm getting anxious about that.

Dr. Miller: Now you're pretty sure there's something really bad, wrong, or something really wrong with you. Is that it?

Ann: Yeah. This need for attention is something I've always had since I was really little. So, like, "You've been messed up for years, Girl."

Dr. Miller: What is the negative belief you have about yourself that makes you feel that you're not worthy of attention?

Ann: That I'm not worthy of attention?

Dr. Miller: Is there some kind of memory from your childhood that reminds you?

Ann: Yeah. On my fifth birthday, my father told me I was nothing special and that I'd be alone forever and that I was unlovable.

Dr. Miller: That sounds really painful. What color is the pain?

Ann: Dark. I guess, black.

Dr. Miller: Dark? Black with darkness?

Ann: "Darkness" is how I would describe it.

Dr. Miller: Darkness—absence of light more than black; right?

Ann: Yeah.

Dr. Miller: Where do you see it in your body?

Ann: My stomach.

Dr. Miller: Let's release it.

Ann releases the black particles of pain with the P/TRP.

Ann: I feel light again.

Dr. Miller: When you think back to that memory, what comes up for you now?

Ann: More anger than pain.

Dr. Miller: Is there still some pain left?

Ann: Yeah. But I think that's more connected to anger at my father, not really that memory specifically. There's pain connected with the anger, I suppose, underneath the anger.

Dr. Miller: You're angry with your father because—"What kind of person tells their daughter this?"

Ann: Then it fucks her over for the rest of her life. Sorry. He's an idiot. Apparently, I have a lot of anger coming up right now.

Dr. Miller: Underneath that anger is a lot of hurt?

Ann: Yup.

Dr. Miller: What color is the hurt?

Ann: Blue.

Dr. Miller: Where is it in the body?

Ann: In my heart.

Dr. Miller: Let's clear it.

Ann releases the blue particles of pain with the P/TRP.

Ann: I think I might need a little more prompting on that one. I still feel it.

Dr. Miller: Where do you feel it?

Ann: In my heart.

Dr. Miller: Is it the same blue?

Ann: No. It's darker.

Dr. Miller: What's happened is that things have shifted a little bit. You released one pain that was related to that previous blue, and now there's another pain. What is this pain in regards to?

Ann: Abandonment.

Dr. Miller: Abandonment.

Ann: I've been left to do everything by myself, I suppose.

Dr. Miller: That you what?

Ann: Just being forced to figure everything else out on my own.

Dr. Miller: Breathe into the darker blue in your heart and feel it like a thick fog. If it's too thick, liquefy it and see it coming right out of your body, right out the pores of your skin.

Ann releases the dark blue particles of pain with the P/TRP.

Dr. Miller: All gone?

Ann: Yeah.

Dr. Miller: How's the anger? Not there?

Ann: I feel okay. I actually feel calm too.

Dr. Miller: Just to reevaluate, how do you feel about the event when you were five years old?

Ann: Right now?

Dr. Miller: Mm-hmm.

Ann: Nothing. Just like it didn't happen to me, I guess. It was just another story.

Dr. Miller: Anger with your father is pretty much gone now? Abandonment?

Ann: Yeah. I'm thinking I'm probably still going to have anger for him. That's probably going to be a work in progress. I don't really feel abandonment, I guess, from him. I'm still a little bit angry. I don't feel it right now, but I know, in my head—

Dr. Miller: Have I explained the difference between formative and non-formative pain?

Ann: Stuff that'll change, yes. Formative pain is stuff that changes you and changes your patterns?

Dr. Miller: You've got it. These are very formative. It's hard to know exactly how things are going to change. You may think you are going to be angry in your future, and you may not. On the other hand, your father was a real jerk. [Laughs] Right?

Ann: Right.

Dr. Miller: We'll see. I'm sure there's a lot of other events that you may have to deal with.

Ann: Can I take it moment by moment, then? Is that how this process, kind of—

Dr. Miller: That's a good question. I don't really know. It could be that things like the abandonment—that the feeling builds on itself and then, when you clear it, a whole bunch of stuff clears at once. We'll just see.

How do you feel about your boyfriend, where we started?

Ann: I don't feel anything, but I do miss him. It's not like a pain—loss of breath.

Dr. Miller: We'll see how much we need to take this up next time because there may be other—what's happening is that the event on Valentine's Day was so powerful for you because you felt the need to feel special, and he made you feel very, very special. You created a fixated memory about that.

By processing all the way through, we certainly reduced your missing him a lot. The question now is this—and I think you already said this—is there may be another event when he made you feel very special as well. It could be we need to pass through the same thing with that event as well. We'll pick up on this next week.

Ann: Sounds great. Thank you.

Dr. Miller: You're welcome.

ImTT Press, publisher

Ann: Releasing the Pain and Attachment After the Breakup of a Relationship-Session #2

Ann reports that, after her last session, she no longer experienced the "intense pain" feeling that she had been living with that came from the breakup of her relationship with her ex-boyfriend, but that all is still not well. In addition to the feeling of "being special" linked with a specific memory of her ex-boyfriend that was processed in the last session, there is an entirely different memory of "'being special" that is still tugging at her heart. That feeling-state was the focus on this session utilizing the FSAP and the P/TRP.

During the processing of the FS, other feelings surface that interfere with the processing of the FS. These feelings are then identified and processed with the P/TRP. Once these feelings are processed, the processing of the FS is continued and completed. Other feelings are also processed as they arise. This transcript illustrates how the FSAP and the P/TRP can be interwoven during treatment.

Dr. Miller: Let's start where we left off last time—which had to do with your ex-boyfriend.

Ann: Yes.

Dr. Miller: How does that feel to you now? Did you miss him?

Ann: I missed him, yeah. I still got a little teary-eyed when thinking about him, but there wasn't the physical sensation, if that makes sense.

Dr. Miller: It's a lot less intense?

Ann: Yeah. I wasn't like I was in pain, but every night before going to sleep, it's just—I don't know. The floodworks turn on or—I don't know.

Dr. Miller: What memory do you have now that is the most intense positive memory that you have of him?

Ann: It was just when we were cuddling on the couch together and he does the whole, run your fingers through your hair. I don't normally let people touch my hair. I just liked it when he did that. That's what's coming to mind.

Dr. Miller: When he's doing that, how does it make you feel about yourself?

Ann: Like I'm cared for, and I felt special.

Dr. Miller: Felt special?

Ann: Mm-hmm.

                                       ImTT Press, publisher

Dr. Miller: On a 0-to-10 scale, when you really let yourself feel—you're lying on the couch, he's running his fingers through your hair—how intensely do you feel special?

Ann: On a 0-to-10 scale, I'd say it's a 7.

Dr. Miller: Where do you feel it in your body?

Ann: The "specialness" in my body? In my gut.

Dr. Miller: So now imagine that you're lying on a couch, he's holding you, and he's running his fingers through your hair, and you feel very, very special.

BLS — Eye Movements

Dr. Miller: Is it increasing, decreasing, or staying the same?

Ann: Decreasing, but slightly—

Dr. Miller: Get into it again.

BLS — Eye Movements

Ann: Kind of stayed the same, but I feel that it's in my chest now, instead of my gut.

Dr. Miller: Stay with that.

BLS — Eye Movements

Dr. Miller: What do you feel now? Is it still "special"?

Ann: Like a yearning.

Dr. Miller: What number would you put it at?

You're lying on the couch, he's holding you, running his fingers through your hair. How that does feel now? At what number would you put it?

Ann: For special? Like a 5-1/2.

Dr. Miller: Okay. Stay with that.

BLS — Eye Movements

Ann: It's about the same. But I had a hard time concentrating on that one. My mind is wandering.

Dr. Miller: Where is it wandering to?

Ann: Just "Don't cry, Ann" and "You don't need him."

Dr. Miller: Okay.

Ann: I'm starting to feel a little anxious.

Dr. Miller: Because?

Ann: I don't want to cry.

Dr. Miller: Why don't you want to cry?

Ann: Because I'm sick of crying over him.

Dr. Miller: Is there some other memory that's more powerful that makes you miss him?

Ann: Not really. I feel like I just "have" him. It's like an entity in my mind that's like ever-consuming. It's not really memories or—

Dr. Miller: If you have him, then what? What will it mean?

Ann: I have a best friend?

Dr. Miller: If you have a best friend, what does it mean about you?

Ann: That I'm not alone and that there's someone I can share time with.

ImTT Press, publisher

Dr. Miller: Deep down inside, you know you are alone, aren't you? It really hurts, doesn't it? What color is that pain?

Ann: Black.

Dr. Miller: Where is that located in your body?

Ann: In my chest.

Dr. Miller: Let's release it.

Ann releases the black particles of pain with the P/TRP.

Dr. Miller: How is the yearning?

Ann: Much more reduced.

Dr. Miller: Do you still see him as your best friend?

Ann: No.

Dr. Miller: Now what are you yearning?

Ann: I'm still mourning the loss of him, it feels like.

Dr. Miller: Let's go back to the lying on the couch. How does that feel to you now?

Ann: That "special"? Like a 4.9.

Dr. Miller: Let's pick up there. You've got it?

Ann: Yes.

BLS — Eye Movements (5 sets)

Ann: Zero.

Dr. Miller: How is that yearning?

Ann: I still feel the yearning, but it's not for Jim.

Dr. Miller: Who's the yearning for?

Ann: I don't know. I just guess that need to connect.

Dr. Miller: This is an over-need that's built up for years. This is why, with Jim—because you had that super intense need to connect—that, when you finally got it—"boom," it created a fixated memory, the feeling-state. Okay?

Ann: Okay.

Dr. Miller: What we want to do is reduce that hyper-need, that over-need to "connect," down to an adult, healthy level.

What I want you to do is let yourself feel that general need to "connect." What number would you put it at?

Ann: A 10.

Dr. Miller: Where do you feel it in your body?

Ann: All over.

BLS — Eye movements

Dr. Miller: What's coming up for you now?

Ann: I don't know. I just keep thinking I just want to be loved.

Dr. Miller: It's really painful that you're not loved, isn't it? What color is that pain?

Ann: Dark. I don't really know what color.

 ImTT Press, publisher

Dr. Miller: Where is it located?

Ann: In my heart.

Dr. Miller: Let's release it.

Ann releases the dark particles of pain with the P/TRP.

Ann: All cleared.

Dr. Miller: When you think about not being loved, how does that feel to you now?

Ann: Honestly? Fuck everyone.

Dr. Miller: What's that? [Laughs]

Ann: My mouth got the best of me.

Dr. Miller: Do you have a negative belief about yourself now?

Ann: I've always had a negative belief about myself.

Dr. Miller: About not being loved? That you don't deserve to be loved? Anything like that?

Ann: I'm just unlovable.

Dr. Miller: When you think back in your life, is there a particular memory that makes you feel unlovable?

Ann: Yeah. My fourth birthday. My dad told me that I was worthless and unlovable and—

Dr. Miller: What's the emotion you have?

Ann: Now it's always coming up as anger, but I believe that underneath it all is a pain, for, when I think about it, I get pissed off.

Dr. Miller: You think what?

Ann: When I think of that and—

Dr. Miller: When you remember that event, how intense is it?

Ann: It's not that intense. I don't really feel it. I barely remember it. I just remember sitting on my bed, and I had just gotten dressed by myself for the first time. Then he came in and told me that and then left the room.

Dr. Miller: So that event is pretty faded now?

Ann: Yeah.

Dr. Miller: Do you still believe that you're unlovable?

Ann: I don't think I'm unlovable, but I don't think that—I don't know. I don't think— maybe I'm not worthy of love. That's what I think.

Dr. Miller: Is there some event in your life that makes you feel that you're not worthy of love?

Ann: I don't know. I haven't always been the best girlfriend growing up, so maybe— I don't know.

Dr. Miller: This is about later on in life, then, that you're not worthy of love is what you're telling me. Can you give me an example of not having been a good girlfriend.

Ann: I've cheated when I was really, really young. I cheated on my first boyfriend. Then I didn't really feel guilty about it. I was 16, 17. My next boyfriend after that had OCD and would randomly go off and tell me that I needed to be punished for my behavior and I'm a horrible girlfriend and my past is just so bad that—

ImTT Press, publisher

Dr. Miller: Your past is so bad?

Ann: Yeah. That's the best I can come up with for now. I don't know.

Dr. Miller: When you say to yourself, "I'm unworthy of being loved," how intense is that now?

Ann: It's not really that intense right now. Maybe just because we cleared all that unlovable—

Dr. Miller: So what you're telling me is that these are the thoughts you've had about yourself in the past but that they're not really very energized anymore.

Ann: No.

Dr. Miller: Which also means that event from the four-year-old is also pretty clear. Is that it?

Ann: Yeah. I can't really think of anything in particular. I have a lot of negative self-talk and constantly—to my roommate, my ex, I'll be like, "Am I pretty? Am I going to be alone forever?"—just randomly.

He's like, "No, Ann. I think you're going to find someone someday."

But it's just all the time. It's just—

Dr. Miller: Did you do that this last week?

Ann: Oh, yeah. Yeah, I did. Not, usually, a week goes by—I don't know. Maybe I'm just obsessed with myself. I don't know.

Dr. Miller: We're only obsessed with ourselves when we're in pain. Think about if you had a stone in your shoe. You're going to be obsessed with the pain until you get the stone out. Same thing. When you're not in pain, you'll stop thinking about yourself.

Let's look at the thought that you're never going to find anybody.

Ann: That's a horrible thought.

Dr. Miller: Does that feel really painful?

Ann: Yes.

Dr. Miller: What color is the pain?

Ann: Black.

Dr. Miller: Where is it located?

Ann: My whole torso.

Dr. Miller: Let's release the pain.

Ann: Okay.

Ann releases the black particles of pain with the P/TRP.

Ann: I'm clear.

Dr. Miller: How does it feel now that no one's ever going to love you?

Ann: Artificial insemination—I'm so glad it's a thing.

Dr. Miller: What do you mean by that?

Ann: Because I really want kids.

Dr. Miller: [Laughs] Screw them; right?

Ann: Yeah, screw them.

Dr. Miller: [Laughs]

Ann: I'm okay with it. It seems okay.

Dr. Miller: Let's go back to what we originally started with, which was Jim. How does that feel to you now?

Ann: Nothing. You can say his name, and it doesn't even—

Dr. Miller: [Laughs]

Ann: It's okay.

Dr. Miller: No yearning?

Ann: There's a slight yearning.

Dr. Miller: For him or a connection?

Ann: Let me try and figure that out.

It's for him. I'm denying myself by telling myself it's not.

Dr. Miller: Make up a scenario that satisfies that yearning with him.

Ann: He would call me when he gets back from Europe and he'd want to see me and I could tell him "No," and then I'd feel a lot better. That's the perfect scenario.

I'd probably get talked into it, and then I'd regret it after I saw him. That's how, in my head, it would work out unrealistically.

Dr. Miller: So you're not really wanting him, are you? What are you really wanting?

Ann: Is him to want me.

Dr. Miller: If he wants you—

Ann: Then I'm special. Goddamn it. I can't get away from that.

Dr. Miller: Let's do that scenario. He's wanting to call you up and you can say, "No," and then you get to feel desired and special; right?

Ann: And I get the control back.

Dr. Miller: This is about control, isn't it?

Ann: A little bit.

Dr. Miller: Feel that control now. What number would you put it at?

Ann: An 8.

Dr. Miller: Where do you feel it in your body?

Ann: All over.

Dr. Miller: Okay.

BLS — Eye Movements

Ann: Zero

Dr. Miller: Can you feel your general need to control?

Ann: Not right now, no.

Dr. Miller: Do you have a negative belief about yourself that makes you feel that you're out of control or you don't have control?

Ann: Sometimes I think I'm crazy and insane, but that's just being a girl.

Dr. Miller: When you think of Jim again, re-evaluate the yearning.

Ann: I don't feel a yearning. I don't.

That's weird.

Dr. Miller: A relief? [Laughs]

Ann: That's pretty awesome. This is awesome. I'm going to sleep tonight.

Dr. Miller: I'll see you next week.

Ann: Awesome.

Carol: Connection Through Sex

(Joining Through Negative Beliefs)

"Intergenerational Joining" is an intense desire to connect with a person that can result in a compulsive behavior based on a person's negative beliefs. For example, if John's father thinks John is a loser, John may connect with his father by being a loser. The following transcript illustrates this dynamic and the use of the FSAP and the P/TRP to resolve it.

Carol: There's something that I want to talk about, but I don't know how comfortable I feel because it's not something I'm proud of in myself. I've been rather promiscuous in the last six months.

I continue to try to stop it because I'm not proud of it, but it fixes what I'm feeling at the moment of feeling alone. It's easy. And then I can just leave, and I don't have to deal with anything. But then, when it's just me when I get home, I feel disgusting and sick of myself. Then when they text me nonstop, I just hate myself for even letting that ever happen. I continuously try to stop, but I can't stop. I'm so ashamed. That's about what's been happening all week. It's part of the reason I've been staying out is just to go see these gentlemen. I don't know why I do it to myself.

Dr. Miller: Why don't we find out? Part of what you said is avoidance? To avoid a feeling; right? But it sounds also like there's a bit of a compulsion there. Does it feel like that? Like you're driven to do it?

Carol: It's disgusting. It's like a coping strategy. Like, "Okay, I guess I don't have to sit at home alone. I can go have fun."

I don't know if it's, like, a compulsion because I say "No" multiple times a week. But it's, like, the other few nights a week that I don't say "No" and I'll be, like, "Okay, I'll come over"—my phone is constantly blowing up. And every time I have it, it's like I feel more and more down on myself. Like, "Why do you let them treat you like this?"

But then, before you know it, I'm letting them treat me like that again.

Dr. Miller: When you say "treat you like that," what does that mean?

Carol: When I'm just walking—just a walking hole, just someone to be with for the night. They don't see me. They don't care about me.

If I wanted them to care about me, I would make that a priority from the beginning and be, like, "If you want to see me, you take me out"—or not just make it purely sexual.

ImTT Press, publisher

Dr. Miller: You're saying that it's about, when you're home alone and you're feeling really, really, really lonely and you just have to do something to get away from the feeling of being alone?

Carol: Yeah. Or just a connection or just—"What's so bad to connect? I love connecting to people." But I—

Dr. Miller: What's interesting here is you're saying you love connecting with people, but that's not what you're doing, is it?

Carol: No.

Dr. Miller: We are dealing with a compulsion. Let's actually identify it exactly. What's happening here is that you have the feeling of need for connection.

   Is that the feeling that seems to be really driving you? The need for connection? When you think of all the behavior, where's the point where you get that feeling?

Carol: When you're talking to them and getting to know them and relating in conversation. That's the best way that I connect.

Dr. Miller: You're going over there, and you start talking with them. Is that it?

Carol: A little bit, but not—no, not really.

Dr. Miller: Where is it that you feel that connection?

Carol: With the gentlemen that I—

Dr. Miller: Yes.

Carol: There is none. There isn't really—I don't get it from the sexual intercourse, but it's more than—it's better than nothing.

Dr. Miller: Okay.

Carol: I like having friends, but with my work, I work with disabled adults. There are no people my age there. At school, there are a few people my age, but everyone's so busy.

There are two girls I might see on occasion. I miss having friends or family to talk to. I'm alone. At least someone wants to see me, even if it's not for the reason that I want to be seen. I'm just so ashamed. I'm disgusted with it.

Dr. Miller: Can you think of a time when sex was really linked with feeling connected?

Carol: In all my relationships—yeah, a really strong connection.

Dr. Miller: Was there one in particular where sex and connection felt really strong?

Carol: Not really one particular—like two, in particular.

Dr. Miller: There are two, in particular?

Carol: Yeah.

Dr. Miller: We're going to need to change protocols here.

Carol: Okay.

Dr. Miller: We'll go back to using the FSAP again. I have to explore this from both directions. We'll start with this one, and we'll see how far it takes us, and then we'll go to the other one eventually.

   What's the most powerful memory you have linking sex and connection?

Carol: That's a tough question.

ImTT Press, publisher

Dr. Miller: You're having difficulty with that? Let's do it differently. I want you to make it up—a scenario of sex and connection.

Carol: That was easy.

Dr. Miller: Can you tell me a little bit about what's going on?

Carol: He's a very handsome man. Just a lot of touching and very sensual—telling me I'm pretty, kissing on the shoulders and—just really loving and appreciating each other and then great sex.

Dr. Miller: When you really let yourself think of that fantasy, what number would you put it? On a 0-to-10 scale intensity?

Carol: A 9.

Dr. Miller: All right. Where do you feel it in your body?

Carol: My gut.

Dr. Miller: Open your eyes, and we'll begin.

BLS — Eye Movements

Carol: It's increased because all I can think about is what my dad told me when I was four years old.

(Intensity of Carol's feeling is no longer a measure of a positive feeling but a negative feeling.)

Carol: Now, I'm freaking out that, if I'll be with my promiscuous side, then I'll never be loved—just like my father told me—that that was the only way I'll ever feel love from a man is if I spread my legs and—that was my first sex talk—now I'm freaking out that I'm never going to be loved.

Dr. Miller: It sounds really painful.

Carol: Yeah. This sucks.

Dr. Miller: What color is that pain?

Carol: Red.

Dr. Miller: Where is it located?

Carol: All over. I don't know. All of me.

Dr. Miller: Let's release it.

Carol releases the red particles of pain with the P/TRP.

Carol: Clear now. I can feel numb or, like, fluffy.

Dr. Miller: You feel what?

Carol: Numb or, like, fluffy—one of the two.

Dr. Miller: Your father told you that a man would only want you to have sex?

Carol: Yes. At the same time he told me I'm worthless and unlovable—

Dr. Miller: At 4? When you were 4?

Carol: Yeah. It was my birthday.

Dr. Miller: You didn't tell me about that part.

Carol: I don't tell anybody.

Dr. Miller: It's not something you want to tell anybody; right?

Carol: I'm ashamed.

ImTT Press, publisher

Dr. Miller: How do you feel about yourself now?

Carol: I hate myself because I was—basically, he gave me my future. The man I hate the most prescribed me my future. I hate that I completely did exactly what he said.

Dr. Miller: Do you know why?

Carol: Because I love him. It sucks.

Dr. Miller: Yeah. That's your way of connecting with him.

Why don't we do something about it.

Carol: Okay.

Dr. Miller: With his talk that nobody is going to want you, there's also a powerful feeling of connection with him. Can you feel it?

Carol: I guess. Like "the old lecture from my dad."

Dr. Miller: You can feel that powerful connection? What I want you to do is focus on that very powerful connection that you have with him and simultaneously focus on that talk.

How intense would you put it, when you really let yourself get into the feeling of being connected with him and the talk?

Carol: I can put that at a 10.

Dr. Miller: A 10?

Carol: Yeah.

Dr. Miller: Where do you feel it in your body?

Carol: My gut.

BLS — Eye Movements

Carol: Zero.

Dr. Miller: How do you feel?

Carol: That my dad's an idiot. Yeah, that's pretty much how I feel. I'm still a little angry at myself. That's something that I know I can work on.

Dr. Miller: Because what?

Carol: I'm still feeling angry at myself, but I know that that's something I can work on—that only I can change myself.

Dr. Miller: You're angry at yourself because?

Carol: I fell into stupid—like, basically, doing what he told me.

Dr. Miller: Yeah. You should have known better at 4 years old, absolutely.

Carol: I should know better at 35.

Dr. Miller: You didn't know you were doing it, that's why.

Carol: Who says that to a 4-year-old?

Dr. Miller: Yeah.

Carol: Hopefully, now, it's not—I've cleared the power of it all. I just want to punch him in the face if I ever see him again.

Dr. Miller: Sounds reasonable to me.

ImTT Press, publisher

ImTT Press, publisher

APPENDIX

162

ImTT Press, publisher

What is the Feeling-State Image Protocol® And How Does It Work?

What you should know about addiction and the FSIP®

Q: What is the Feeling-State Image Protocol (FSIP)?

A: The Feeling-State Theory of Addiction states that addictions are caused by a fixated memory called a feeling-state (FS). The FS is created when a positive event is so intense that the memory of that event becomes fixated in the mind. Composed of the memory of the sensations, emotions, thoughts, and behavior of that event, the FS, whenever it is activated, creates the urges and cravings to do the behavior contained within the fixated memory.

For example, a social gambler won a large hand playing poker. The experience of winning was so intense for him that an FS was created which consisted of the feeling of excitement and the thought "I am a winner." From that point on, he became a compulsive gambler. Even though he lost over $1 million over 10 years, the fixated memory— the FS—did not change. He kept chasing that feeling of being a winner, even though he had lost so much money.

The major difference between behavioral addictions, such as a gambling compulsion, and substance addictions, such as cocaine, is that psychoactive drugs can create their own FS. For example, cocaine can produce an intense feeling of euphoria. The feeling of euphoria can be so strong that an FS is immediately created.

The Feeling-State Image Protocol (FSIP) eliminates addictions by eliminating the FS. Once the FS is gone, there is nothing left to cause the urges and cravings of the addiction. Compulsive gamblers can gamble again, compulsive shoppers can shop, and sex addicts can have sex without triggering the previously addictive behavior. However, when dealing with psychoactive substances, since the psychoactive substance itself can create an immediate FS, abstinence is necessary is order to make sure the FS is not recreated. Since the urges and cravings to use the substance are no longer present, this will not be difficult.

ImTT Press, publisher

List of ASFs Embedded in Feeling-States

Any ASF can become the feeling embedded in a feeling-state. The following list is necessarily incomplete but does consist of the feelings most commonly embedded in an FS. I have included phrases like "big man on campus" because these kinds of phrases are often the way people articulate the ASF.

ASFs are divided into four categories: safety, relational, winning (status), and sensation-alive. Some ASFs, especially the ones expressed as phrases, may stimulate feelings in more than one category. For example, the ASF "bonding" may trigger feelings of both relational and safety. "Invincible" may include categories of safety, relational, and winning. For the purpose of treatment, processing the FS does not require distinguishing between these categories. However, Phase 4 processing of the underlying NC may require a more nuanced understanding of the FS in order to identify the NC.

Safety:

safe, secure

Relational:

bonding, connected, important, special, powerful, strong, invincible, acknowledged, "I exist," "cared for," whole

Winning (status):

"the man," "big man on campus," feminine, masculine, smart, winner, approval, reward, "I can have what I want"

Sensation-Alive:

excitement, danger, aliveness, euphoria, alive

What feelings are NOT the feelings embedded in a Feeling-State

Not every positive feeling is an FS. As explained in the text, the only feelings embedded in the FS are assured-survival feelings (ASF). While people will often state that the following feelings are how they feel after enacting the addictive behavior, these feelings are actually the result of the person experiencing the ASF, not the feeling that is embedded in the FS and therefore should not be processed as part of an FS.

All ASFs are feelings that are self-referential. ASFs are never about a person's feeling for another person. ASFs are always feelings about the self.

NOT Assured-Survival Feelings:

comfort, relaxation, peaceful, calm, excitement (anticipatory)
urges, cravings, non-self-referential feelings, the feeling of love for another person, wanting to hang onto a person, emotions such as "happy" and "joy" are never ASFs.

                                                                     ImTT Press, publisher

ImTT Press, publisher

The following questions and answers
can be used as an informational brochure for a client.

Permission is granted to copy these pages
as a handout for clients.

You may use the brochure for either the FSIP or FSAP.

What is the
Feeling-State Addiction Protocol®
and
How Does It Work?

What you should know about addiction and the FSAP®

Q: What is the Feeling-State Addiction Protocol (FSAP)?

A: The Feeling-State Theory of Addiction states that addictions are caused by a fixated memory called a feeling-state (FS). The FS is created when a positive event is so intense that the memory of that event becomes fixated in the mind. Composed of the memory of the sensations, emotions, thoughts, and behavior of that event, the FS, whenever it is triggered, creates the urges and cravings to do the behavior contained within the fixated memory.

For example, a social gambler won a large hand playing poker. The experience of winning was so intense for him that an FS was created which consisted of the feeling of "I am a winner" linked with playing poker. From that point on, he became a compulsive gambler. Even though he lost over $1 million over 10 years, the fixated memory—the FS—did not change. He kept chasing that feeling of being a winner, even though he had lost so much money.

The major difference between behavioral addictions, such as a gambling compulsion, and substance addictions, such as cocaine, is that psychoactive drugs can create their own FSs. For example, cocaine can produce an intense feeling of euphoria. The feeling of euphoria can be so strong that an FS is immediately created.

The Feeling-State Addiction Protocol (FSAP) eliminates addictions by eliminating the FS. Once the FS is gone, there is nothing left to cause the urges and cravings of the addiction. Compulsive gamblers can gamble again, compulsive shoppers can shop, and sex addicts can have sex—all without triggering what had been their previous addictive behavior. However, when dealing with psychoactive substances, since a psychoactive substance itself can create an immediate FS, abstinence is necessary in order to make sure a new FS is not created. Since the urges and cravings to use the substance are no longer present, this will be much easier than your previous experiences.

ImTT Press, publisher

Q: What does this mean for me?

A: Once the FS is eliminated, the previously addictive behavior does not need to be managed or controlled. You will not have the urges, cravings, irritability, and frustration that have likely been part of your previous attempts to quit. Encountering what previously would have been triggers for the behavior just won't bother you anymore; previous triggers will no longer activate the addictive behavior because there will not be an FS to activate.

Q: In the past, when I quit doing one addictive behavior, I would just start doing another. Is this "quitting" any different?

A: Yes. This is different. In the past, if you just stopped doing an addictive behavior without eliminating the underlying FS, you wouldn't have had an opportunity to resolve the underlying cause of the addiction; so another behavior had become attached to the FS. Eliminating the FS means that "quitting" will not result in switching addictive behaviors.

Q: What will my therapist ask me to do?

A: Your therapist will ask you to identify the feeling that underlies the behavior. This is a very crucial step. The therapist will guide you through identifying the exact part of the behavior that has the most intensity and the feeling linked with that behavior.

Q: How many sessions will it take?

A: Most addictions are eliminated within five to six sessions. More or fewer sessions may be required, depending on the number of FSs associated with the addictive behavior.

Q: More than one feeling?

A: Yes. Some addictive behaviors can have two or even three FSs linked with the same addictive behavior. After each FS is eliminated, you will notice a reduction in the intensity or frequency of your cravings and urges.

Q: What do I have to do between sessions?

A: Your therapist will give you homework to help you discover if you still feel urges and cravings to do the addictive behavior. Doing your homework will uncover if there are more FSs to be eliminated. Reporting this honestly is important so that the FSs (and the addictive behavior they create) can be completely eliminated.

Q: How does the FSAP therapy work?

A: FSAP is a modified form of Eye Movement Desensitization and Reprocessing (EMDR). EMDR has been proven effective in the treatment of Posttraumatic Stress Disorder (PTSD). FSAP uses the bilateral stimulation approach of EMDR—such as eye movements—but differs from the standard EMDR protocol by focusing on the positive feelings underlying the addictive behavior.

Q: Once the addictive behavior is eliminated, do I need any further therapy?

A: Feeling-states are often created because there is an intense psychological desire for that feeling. Resolving these predisposing emotional problems can prevent problems farther down the road.

For more information, go to www.FSAProtocol.com

ImTT Press, publisher

Q: What does this mean for me?

A: Once the FS is eliminated, the previously addictive behavior does not need to be managed or controlled. You will not have the urges, cravings, irritability, and frustration that have likely been part of your previous attempts to quit. Encountering what previously would have been triggers for the behavior just won't bother you anymore; the previous triggers will no longer act as triggers because there are no FSs to be triggered.

Q: In the past, when I quit doing one addictive behavior, I would just start doing another. Is this "quitting" any different?

A: Yes, this is different. If you just stop doing an addictive behavior without eliminating the underlying FS, you won't have resolved the cause of the addiction; so another behavior becomes attached to the FS. Eliminating the FS means that "quitting" will not result in switching addictive behaviors.

Q: What will my therapist ask me to do?

A: Your therapist will ask you to identify the feeling that underlies the behavior. This is a very crucial step. The therapist will guide you into identifying the exact part of the behavior that has the most intensity and the feeling linked with that behavior.

Q: How many sessions will it take?

A: Most addictions are eliminated within 5-6 sessions. The number of sessions will vary according to the number of FSs associated with the addictive behavior and any additional traumas or memories that may need to be processed as well.

Q: More than one feeling?

A: Yes. Some addictive behaviors can have two or even three FSs linked with the same addictive behavior. After each FS is eliminated, you will notice a reduction in the intensity of your cravings and urges.

Q: What do I have to do between sessions?

A: Your therapist will give you homework to help you discover if you still feel urges and cravings to do the addictive behavior. Doing your homework will uncover if there are more FSs to be eliminated. Reporting this honestly is important so that the FSs (and the addictive behavior they create) can be completely eliminated.

Q: Once the addictive behavior is eliminated, do I need any further therapy?

A: Feeling-states are often created because there is an intense psychological desire for that feeling. Resolving these predisposing emotional problems can prevent problems farther down the road.

For more information, go to www.imttherapy.com

General Instructions for the Image Transformation Therapy Protocols

The following protocols provide a thorough release of the images creating dysfunctional feelings and behaviors. However, developing the appropriate targets is essential. This requires a deeper understanding of ImTT and the Survival Model of Psychological Dynamics. For more specific scripts targeting different issues, see the manual, *Image Transformation Therapy Scripts for Therapists* by Robert Miller (2016).

The Pain/Terror Release Protocol

The P/TRP utilizes a breathing/visualization technique. This process works best if, when the color is visualized, it is thought of as an actual physical substance being removed from the body. Breathing the color out (releasing the color) is easier if the color is visualized as composed of tiny, tiny, tiniest particles of a size that easily flows out of the body. Alternately, if the person conceives of the P/T as a sound, the sound should be thought of as being composed of tiny units that somehow diminish to no sound. Whether you use a visual or auditory mode of identifying the P/T, it is very important to think of the color or sounds as an actual substance that is being released from the body. The more intensely this process can be visualized or represented in a sensory modality, the more complete the release of the P/T will be. The more complete the release, the more complete the transformation of the memories, feelings, and behaviors.

<u>IMPORTANT!</u>

Ideally, the process of the P/TRP moves seamlessly from identifying the event to identifying the feeling about the event to identifying the color (sound) of the P/T. Once the color of the P/T has been identified, it is no longer necessary to pay any attention to the event, the feeling, or the P/T. Instead, the focus is to hone in on the color (or sound) of the P/T that has been identified, functionally ignoring the P/T's roots until, at the very end, when all color (or sound) is gone and there is an instruction to re-assess the feeling about the originating event.

170

ImTT Press, publisher

The Pain/Terror Release Protocol Instructions

The Pain/Terror Release Protocol (P/TRP) releases the pain/terror (P/T) associated with disturbing memories, negative feelings, and/or negative thoughts. If you are using sound as a way to identify the P/T, substitute the word "sound" for the word "color."

The parts of the body chosen in this protocol for the release have been generally found to be effective. As you become more adept at this process, you may find that the colors are mostly focused in certain parts of the body and not others. Therefore, you may want to emphasize those areas. However, you can never really know ahead of time when a release from one area of the body will be useful. Therefore, the entire protocol should be performed every time.

Another important part of the protocol is to see the color as composed of very tiny, tiny, tiny particles. Visualizing the color in this way appears to make the release easier. If the client uses sound instead of color, find an image in which the general image is composed of very small units such as small units of sound. The image does not have to be reasonable. The image just has to make sense to the client.

While this protocol can be done at home by the client, the problem that most people seem to have is that the mind wanders and tends to lose focus on releasing the particles. A recording of the protocol can be made by the therapist and given to the client to use at home to help overcome the wandering-mind problem so that the client can remain focused on releasing the color particles completely from all parts of the body.

The only purpose of the P/TRP is to release the P/T and transform the behavior and feelings. If the client finds focusing on different areas of the body or visualizing the color in different ways is more effective, go with what works for the client. Sometimes you just might have to get creative in order to get the P/T to release. How will you know if what you're doing is right? If the client's attitude and feelings toward the original memory or feeling undergo a permanent transformation, you're doing the protocol correctly.

Summary of Important Points:

1. The person is only to lightly acknowledge the presence of the pain or terror. Make sure the person understands that he is not to intensely connect with the feelings.

2. Process only one formative event in a session.

3. Do the entire protocol every time if the person can maintain psychological stability.

4. Visualize the color/sound as being composed of small units.

5. If the client becomes stuck in the release, be creative in finding a method of release.

Learning the P/TRP

It is easiest to learn the P/TRP using an event that client remembers as painful. So for the client's first processing with the P/TRP, pick an event that is obviously emotionally painful. This approach makes it easy to identify the pain and allows the client to focus on learning the basics of the protocol.

The following is a script of the instructions for the P/TRP. The script is in italics. The words in brackets are instructions for the therapist. For each part of the body, allow time for at least 3 breaths, though more time can be given as needed.

Some people have difficulty visualizing the color and/or the release of the particles. Sometimes the problem occurs because the person has unrealistic expectations about what he should be "seeing." A simple way around this difficulty is to have the person pretend or imagine the color, the location, and the release. Pretending to "see" the color removes the anxiety of having to visualize.

Non-visualizing approaches to releasing the P/T

Even the pretending-to-see technique does not always work. In this situation, it is important to work with the person to find some approach that will work for them. Instead of color, a sound or a tactile representation of the P/T can be utilized. Work with the person until he can find a way to represent the P/T and release it. The goal is to release the P/T. Exactly how the person releases the P/T is not important. Whatever method works is good.

Releasing the Pain from a Painful Event   (General Instructions)

The following is a general script of the instructions for using the P/TRP.
The script is in *italics*. The words in brackets are instructions for the therapist.
Script: Before we begin, I want you to be very clear about something that is very important for making the treatment easy and gentle. When I ask you about what you feel, I don't want you to get into the feelings. I just want you to kind of notice the feelings from a distance. Okay? If you experience the feelings too much, it actually slows down the release process. Does that make sense to you? Just kind of notice the feelings from a distance. Once I ask you about the color of the feeling, I don't even want you to think of the event, image, or feeling again until we have finished processing and we evaluate the change. Okay? With that in mind, let's begin.

1. *I'm going to ask you to lightly describe that painful memory. Again, I don't want you to get deeply into the pain. Feeling the pain is not necessary. Just be aware that the pain is there. Once the color of the pain is identified, just focus on the color. Don't think of the event or the feeling or the pain again–just the color.*

2. *Now lightly describe the painful memory.*

3. *What color is the pain?*

4. *From now on, I don't want you to think of anything but the color. Forget everything else. Just focus on the color, okay?*

5. *Where is the* [state color] *located in your body?*

6. *Visualize the* [state color] *as being composed of tiny, tiny, little* [state color] *particles.*

7. *Take a slow breath and visualize breathing into the* [state color] *particles.*

8. *As you breathe out, see the tiny* [state color] *particles moving directly out of your body.*

9. *Breathe into the center of your brain and release the tiny* [state color] *particles out the center of your forehead.*

10. *Breathe into the center of your brain and release the tiny* [state color] *particles out your eyes.*

11. *Breathe into your chest and release the tiny* [state color] *particles down your arms and out the palms of your open hands.*

12. *See your spine as being composed of guitar strings that go from the bottom of your spine to the top of your head. Breathe into the guitar strings; and as you breathe out, release the tension on the guitar strings and see the tiny, tiny* [state color] *particles radiate out in all directions as you release the tension on the lower guitar strings.*

13. *See the tiny* [state color] *particles radiate out in all directions as you release the tension on the middle guitar strings.*

14. *See the tiny,* [state color] *particles radiate out in all directions as you release the tension on the upper guitar strings.*

15. *Breathe into your abdomen and release the tiny* [state color] *particles out your navel area.*

16. *Breathe into your abdomen and release the tiny* [state color] *particles down your legs and out the bottoms of your feet.*

17. *See a spot 6 inches below your feet, between your feet...breathe into that spot... and see the tiny* [state color] *particles drain down your body, go through the spot, and be absorbed into the earth...see the* [state color] *particles drain down your body, go through that spot, and be absorbed...absorbed...absorbed into the earth.*

18. *Place your feet flat against the floor. See a six-inch sphere 18 inches beneath your feet. Breathe into the sphere...breathe into the sphere and see the tiny* [state color] *particles release from the sphere...see the tiny, tiny* [state color] *particles releasing from the sphere.*

19. *Breathe into your heart...breathe into your heart and release the tiny, tiny* [state color] *particles out your heart...releasing the tiny* [state color] *particles out of your heart.*

20. *Breathe into the depths of your heart...breathe into the deep, deep depths of your heart and release the tiny, tiny* [state color] *particles from the depths of your heart... releasing the tiny* [state color] *particles from the deep depths of your heart.*

21. *Breathe into your throat...breathe into your throat and release the tiny* [state color] *particles out your throat...releasing the tiny* [state color] *particles out of your throat.*

22. *Breathe into your voice...breathe into the depths of your voice and release the tiny* [state color] *particles from your voice...releasing the tiny* [state color] *particles from the deep depths of your voice.*

23. *Breathe into the right side of your brain...breathe into the right side of your brain and release the tiny, tiny* [state color] *particles out the right side of your brain... releasing the tiny* [state color] *particles out the right side of your brain.*

24. *Breathe into the left side of your brain...breathe into the left side of your brain and release the tiny, tiny* [state color] *particles out the left side of your brain...releasing the tiny* [state color] *particles out the left side of your brain.*

25. *Breathe into the front of your brain...breathe into the front of your brain and release the tiny, tiny* [state color] *particles out the front of your brain...releasing the tiny* [state color] *particles out the front of your brain.*

26. *Breathe into the back of your brain...breathe into the back of your brain and release the tiny, tiny* [state color] *particles out the back of your brain...releasing the tiny* [state color] *particles out the back of your brain.*

ImTT Press, publisher

27. *Breathe into the center of your brain...breathe into the center of your brain and see the tiny, tiny* [state color] *particles, releasing, radiating out in all directions from the center of your brain...see the tiny* [state color] *particles, releasing, radiating out in all directions from the center of your brain.*

28. *Breathe into your mind...breathe into the deep depths of your mind and release the tiny* [state color] *particles from your mind...releasing the tiny* [state color] *particles from the deep depths of your mind.*

29. *Breathe into the core of your self...breathe into what you think of as the core of your self...and release the tiny, tiny* [state color] *particles out the core of your self... releasing the tiny* [state color] *particles out the core of your self.*

30. *Imagine that you are about to yawn. Imagine that you are yawning a deep, wide yawn. As you yawn, see the* [state color] *particles release from the core of your self...as you feel the yawn throughout your whole body...as you feel the yawn throughout your whole body, see the tiny* [state color] *particles releasing from the core of your self.*

31. *Scan your body to see if there are any* [state color] *particles remaining in your body. If there are, breathe into that part of your body and then breathe the tiny* [state color] *particles out the pores of your skin in that area.*

32. *Let's re-evaluate the pain of the memory. Does it feel less charged when you think of the event again?*

33. [If the emotional reaction is acutely painful, if another feeling has surfaced, or if the color has changed, re-evaluate what the person is feeling. If another feeling has surfaced, the P/TRP for that feeling may need to be done.]

34. [If the memory is less charged, do the Image De-Construction Protocol.]

Image De-Construction Protocol

Image De-Construction Protocol (General Instructions)

1. *Visualize the image.* [Or whatever method the client has used to represent the image.]

2. *Now visualize the image as being composed of tiny, tiny particles like pixels on a TV screen.* [Client indicates when this is done.]

3. *Now we are going to deconstruct the image. You can deconstruct the image by dropping the particles to the ground, using a hammer to break up the image, washing the image away, or by using any other method that works for you. Pick a method you like and deconstruct the image. Tell me when you're finished.*
   [Client indicates when this is done.]

4. *Now re-image it again, and tell me how it looks. Is the image as vivid as it was, starting to blur, falling apart, or changing in some way?* [Client describes the image.]

5. *Now pixelate the image again.* [Client indicates when this is done.]

6. *Okay, now deconstruct the image again.* [Client indicates when this is done.]

7. *Now re-image it again, and tell me how it looks.* [Client describes the image.]

8. [Continue with steps 5, 6, and 7 until the image cannot be re-created.]

9. [Once either the image cannot be re-created or a positive image emerges, release the pixel-particles of the image from the body. Allow about 3 breaths per part of the body, though more time can be given as needed.]

10. *Breathe into the center of your brain and release the tiny pixel-particles out the center of your forehead.*

11. *Breathe into the center of your brain and release the tiny pixel-particles out your eyes.*

12. *Breathe into your chest and release the tiny pixel-particles down your arms and out the palms of your open hands.*

13. *See your spine as being composed of guitar strings that go from the bottom of your spine to the top of your head. Breathe into the guitar strings; and as you breathe out, release the tension on the guitar strings and see the tiny pixel-particles radiate out in all directions as you release the tension on the lower guitar strings.*

14. *See the tiny pixel-particles radiate out in all directions as you release the tension on the middle guitar strings.*

15. *See the tiny pixel-particles radiate out in all directions as you release the tension on the upper guitar strings.*

16. *Breathe into your abdomen and release the tiny pixel-particles out your navel area.*

17. *Breathe into your abdomen and release the tiny pixel-particles down your legs and out the bottoms of your feet.*

18. *See a spot 6 inches below your feet, between your feet…breathe into that spot… and see the tiny pixel-particles drain down your body, go through the spot, and be absorbed into the earth…see the tiny pixel-particles drain down your body, go through that spot, and be absorbed…absorbed…absorbed into the earth.*

19. *Place your feet flat against the floor. See a six-inch sphere 18 inches beneath your feet. Breathe into the sphere…breathe into the sphere and see the tiny pixel-particles release from the sphere…see the tiny, tiny pixel-particles releasing from the sphere.*

20. *Breathe into your heart...breathe into your heart and release the tiny pixel-particles out your heart...releasing the tiny pixel-particles out of your heart.*

21. *Breathe into the depths of your heart…breathe into the deep, deep depths of your heart, and release the tiny, tiny pixel-particles from the deep depths of your heart… releasing the tiny pixel-particles from the deep depths of your heart*

22. *Breathe into your throat…breathe into your throat and release the tiny pixel-particles out your throat…releasing the tiny pixel-particles out of your throat.*

23. *Breathe into your voice…breathe into the depths of your voice and release the tiny pixel-particles from your voice…releasing the tiny pixel-particles from the deep depths of your voice.*

24. *Breathe into the right side of your brain...breathe into the right side of your brain and release the tiny, tiny pixel-particles out the right side of your brain...releasing the tiny pixel-particles out the right side of your brain.*

25. *Breathe into the left side of your brain...breathe into the left side of your brain and release the tiny, tiny pixel-particles out the left side of your brain...releasing the tiny pixel-particles out the left side of your brain.*

26. *Breathe into the front of your brain...breathe into the front of your brain and release the tiny, tiny pixel-particles out the front of your brain...releasing the tiny pixel-particles out the front of your brain.*

27. *Breathe into the back of your brain...breathe into the back of your brain and release the tiny, tiny pixel-particles out the back of your brain...releasing the tiny pixel-particles out the back of your brain.*

28. *Breathe into the center of your brain…breathe into the center of your brain and see the tiny, tiny pixel-particles, releasing, radiating out in all directions from the center of your brain...see the tiny pixel-particles, releasing, radiating out in all directions from the center of your brain.*

29. *Breathe into your mind…breathe into the deep depths of your mind and release the tiny pixel-particles from your mind…releasing the tiny pixel-particles from the deep depths of your mind.*

ImTT Press, publisher

30. *Breathe into the core of your self...breathe into what you think of as the core of your self and release the tiny pixel-particles from the core of your self...releasing the tiny pixel-particles from the core of your self.*

31. *Imagine that you are about to yawn. Imagine that you are yawning a deep, wide yawn. As you yawn, see the tiny pixel-particles release from the core of your self...as you feel the yawn throughout your whole body...as you feel the yawn throughout your whole body, see the tiny pixel-particles releasing from the core of your self.*

32. *Scan your body to see if there are any particles remaining in your body. If there are, breathe into that part of your body and then breathe the tiny pixel-particles out the pores of your skin in that area.*

33. *Let's re-evaluate the image. What is your reaction to the image now?*
[There should be some change in attitude toward the image even if some charge remains.]

34. [If the reaction is intensely charged, re-evaluate the situation. There may be another feeling related to the image.]

When there are multiple feelings related to an image or a memory, the image may become less charged or altered in some way without being completely released after one complete processing with the IDP. This may not be noticed until the next session. Then repeat both the P/TRP and the IDP on the memory or image.

ImTT Press, publisher

Changing Patterns Protocol

Having released the P/T, the person's psychological dynamics are now different. He will have a different attitude toward previous memories, feelings, and behavior. However, the old psychological patterns created by the P/T still need to be transformed. This transformation is accomplished by focusing for a short time on significant memories and daily behaviors. When the person focuses on the old patterns, his mind will automatically begin to transform the old thoughts and patterns. Even without doing this technique, the mind would begin this process, but the Changing Patterns technique will accelerate the transformation and make the inner shift smoother.

The following list of areas of the person's life to focus on are just suggestions that might prove useful. The areas to best focus on are the ones that the P/T has most affected. For example, if the P/T of an underlying anger was processed, focusing on the person's interactions with certain people who have often triggered that anger is likely a good place to begin.

After the Image De-Construction Protocol has been completed:

Instructions:

Script: *Now that you've released the image of—(name the event or feeling)— you also need to change the old way of looking at memories and how you see your life changing. For about 15 to 20 seconds, I'm going to ask you to focus your mind on different things. Don't try to do anything but just focus for about 15 to 20 seconds on the different things I suggest to focus on.*

So for 15 to 20 seconds, pick relevant memories for the client to focus on, such as the person who was involved in the event or the situation.

Then after doing several memories, have the person focus on the following, as seems useful:

Now I want you to focus on your life:
- *1 hour from now for 30 seconds...*
- *3 hours from now for 15 seconds...*
- *The next meal... Your evening time... Going to bed... Waking up... Going to work... 2 days from now... 1 week from now... 1 month from now... 1 week ago... 1 month ago... 2 years ago... Your current relationship... Your job...*

ImTT Press, publisher

The Chronic Pain Protocol Instructions

The P/TRP can help with chronic pain. When a person experiences pain for a long time, the sensation of pain builds up in the body. The effect is that the person feels the pain more intensely. Releasing the built-up pain will reduce the sensation of pain. A common occurrence is for the sensation of pain to reduce by half or more. However, because the physical pain is being constantly created, the release of physical pain will have to be done every day to prevent the buildup of the sensation.

A problem that occurs more with physical pain than with a psychological P/T is difficulty releasing the color. Often the color seems to get stuck somewhere. The solution is to think of the tiny color particles as a physical substance that is trying to move through and out the body. Thinking in terms of "How can I drain those particles out of the body?" or "Why are the particles getting stuck?" can guide you to resolving the problems.

Example: Gentry's chronic pain is in his hips. He's been trying to move the particles down his leg, but they seem to get stuck in his knee. A solution may be to visualize the particles leaving out the front of the knee instead of moving down the body. Another possibility is for the person to visualize the particles dissolving and then flowing out. The goal is to creatively find a solution to the blockage.

It is often useful for a person to come up with his/her own creative ways to release the color. When Jerry visualized his pain, he saw it as "compressed." His method of release was to visualize the black color as made up of small particles and then an "avalanche" released the particles. Ruth visualized the pain around her spine as a black rubber band. She released the rubber band by seeing it composed of small particles and the rubber band falling apart. Working with the person to find a creative solution to release the pain will also give them the experience and confidence to utilize the technique at home.

The Chronic Pain Protocol Script

1. *Identify the area of the body that is painful.*

2. *On a 1 - 10 scale, how intense is the pain?*

3. *What color is the pain?*

4. *From now on, I don't want you to think of anything but the color. Forget everything else. Just focus on the color, okay?*

5. *See the color as being composed of tiny, tiny little* [state color] *particles.*

6. *Take a slow breath and visualize the breath going into the color particles.*

7. *Now breathe the* [state color] *particles directly out of your body through the pores of your skin. Visualize the tiny, tiny, tiny* [state color] *particles flowing out of your body. Take your time and find a way to release the* [state color] *particles out that part of your body.*

8. [At this point, have the client release the color particles from whatever exit point is closest to the pain. If the pain is in the shoulder, begin by releasing the particles from the hand. Then release the particles from the elbow down to the arm. This pattern of release clears the path for releasing the color particles from the painful part of the body. Use this same pattern if the pain is located in the hip: begin releasing with the foot and work up the leg.]

9. *Now we are going to release the* [state color] *particles from the closest easy exit point. We are going to start at that exit point so that we can clear the channels; otherwise, some of the particles might get stuck. So breathe into your* [name the exit point, e.g. foot] *and see the tiny* [state color] *particles flow out your* [name the exit point].

10. *Breathe into your* [name a part of the body further from the exit point] *and visualize the* [state color] *particles flowing down your* [name limb–i.e., leg].

11. [Continue with step 10 until you reach the area of the pain.]

12. [After releasing the color particles from the specific area where the pain is experienced, release the color particles from the other parts of the body.]

13. *As the sensation of pain often builds up in other parts of the body, we are going to release these particles from other parts of your body.*

14. *Breathe into the center of your brain and release the tiny* [state color] *particles out the center of your forehead.*

15. *Breathe into the center of your brain and release the tiny* [state color] *particles out your eyes.*

16. *Breathe into your chest and release the tiny* [state color] *particles down your arms and out the palms of your open hands.*

17. *See your spine as being composed of guitar strings that go from the bottom of your spine to the top of your head. Breathe into the guitar strings; and as you breathe out, release the tension on the guitar strings and see the tiny* [state color] *particles radiate out in all directions as you release the tension on the lower guitar strings.*

18. *See the tiny,* [state color] *particles radiate out in all directions as you release the tension on the middle guitar strings.*

19. *See the tiny,* [state color] *particles radiate out in all directions as you release the tension on the upper guitar strings.*

20. *Breathe into your abdomen and release the tiny* [state color] *particles out your navel area.*

21. *Breathe into your abdomen and release the tiny* [state color] *particles down your legs and out the bottoms of your feet.*

22. *See a spot 6 inches below your feet, between your feet…breathe into that spot…and see the tiny* [state color] *particles drain down your body, go through the spot, and be absorbed into the earth…see the tiny* [state color] *particles drain down your body, go through that spot, and be absorbed…absorbed…absorbed into the earth.*

23. *Place your feet flat against the floor. See a six-inch sphere 18 inches beneath your feet. Breathe into the sphere…breathe into the sphere and see the tiny* [state color] *particles release from the sphere…see the tiny, tiny* [state color] *particles releasing from the sphere.*

24. *Breathe into your heart...breathe into your heart and release the tiny* [state color] *particles out your heart...releasing the tiny* [state color] *particles out your heart.*

25. *Breathe into the depths of your heart...breathe into the deep, deep, depths of your heart and release the tiny, tiny* [state color] *particles from the deep depths of your heart...releasing the tiny* [state color] *particles from the deep depths of your heart.*

26. *Breathe into your throat…breathe into your throat and release the tiny* [state color] *particles out your throat…releasing the tiny* [state color] *particles out of your throat.*

27. *Breathe into your voice…breathe into the depths of your voice and release the tiny* [state color] *particles from your voice…releasing the tiny* [state color] *particles from the deep depths of your voice.*

28. *Breathe into the right side of your brain...breathe into the right side of your brain and release the tiny, tiny* [state color] *particles out the right side of your brain...releasing the tiny* [state color] *particles out the right side of your brain.*

29. *Breathe into the left side of your brain...breathe into the left side of your brain and release the tiny, tiny* [state color] *particles out the left side of your brain...releasing the tiny* [state color] *particles out the left side of your brain.*

ImTT Press, publisher

30. *Breathe into the front of your brain...breathe into the front of your brain and release the tiny, tiny* [state color] *particles out the front of your brain...releasing the tiny* [state color] *particles out the front of your brain.*

31. *Breathe into the back of your brain...breathe into the back of your brain and release the tiny, tiny* [state color] *particles out the back of your brain...releasing the tiny* [state color] *particles out the back of your brain.*

32. *Breathe into the center of your brain...breathe into the center of your brain and see the tiny, tiny* [state color] *particles, releasing, radiating out in all directions from the center of your brain...see the tiny* [state color] *particles, releasing, radiating out in all directions from the center of your brain.*

33. *Breathe into your mind...breathe into the deep depths of your mind and release the tiny* [state color] *particles from your mind...releasing the tiny* [state color] *particles from the deep depths of your mind.*

34. *Breathe into the core of your self... breathe into what you think of as the core of your self and release the tiny* [state color] *particles from the core of your self...releasing the tiny* [state color] *particles from the core of your self.*

35. *Imagine that you are about to yawn. Imagine that you are yawning a deep, wide yawn. As you yawn, see the tiny* [state color] *particles release from the core of your self... as you feel the yawn throughout your whole body...as you feel the yawn throughout your whole body, see the tiny* [state color] *particles releasing from the core of your self.*

36. *Scan your body to see if there are any* [state color] *particles left in your body. If there are, breathe into that part of your body and then breathe the tiny* [state color] *particles out the pores of your skin in that area.*

37. *Let's re-evaluate the pain level. On a scale of 1 – 10, how intense is your pain now?*

38. *Is there another color? What is the color?*

39. [Evaluate for other emotions and images that may need to be processed.]

ImTT Press, publisher

Image De-Construction Protocol

Script: *When a person has been in pain a long time, the person often begins to constantly see themselves as a person in pain, which adds to the problem. So what we're going to do is release that image.*

1. *Visualize an image of yourself being in pain.*

2. *Now visualize the image as being composed of tiny, tiny particles like pixels on a TV screen.* [Client indicates when this is done.]

3. *Now we are going to deconstruct the image. You can deconstruct the image by dropping the particles to the ground, using a hammer to break up the image, washing the image away, or by using any other method that works for you. So pick a method you like and deconstruct the image. Tell me when you're finished.* [Client indicates when this is done.]

4. *Now re-image it again, and tell me how it looks. Is it just as intense, beginning to fade, or are parts of the image dropping out?* [Client describes the image.]

5. *Now pixelate the image again.* [Client indicates when this is done.]

6. *Okay, now deconstruct the image again.* [Client indicates when this is done.]

7. *Let's re-evaluate. Now re-image it again, and tell me how it looks.* [Client describes the image.]

8. [Continue with steps 5, 6, and 7 until the image cannot be re-created.]

9. [Once either the image cannot be re-created or a positive image emerges, release the pixel-particles of the image from the body. Allow about 3 breaths per part of the body, though more time can be given as needed.]

10. *Breathe into the center of your brain and release the tiny pixel-particles out the center of your forehead.*

11. *Breathe into the center of your brain and release the tiny pixel-particles out your eyes.*

12. *Breathe into your chest and release the tiny pixel-particles down your arms and out the palms of your open hands.*

13. *See your spine as being composed of guitar strings that go from the bottom of your spine to the top of your head. Breathe into the guitar strings; and as you breathe out, release the tension on the guitar strings and see the tiny pixel-particles radiate out in all directions as you release the tension on the lower guitar strings.*

14. *See the tiny pixel-particles radiate out in all directions as you release the tension on the middle guitar strings.*

15. *See the tiny pixel-particles radiate out in all directions as you release the tension on the upper guitar strings.*

                                                                       ImTT Press, publisher

16. *Breathe into your abdomen and release the tiny pixel-particles out your navel area.*

17. *Breathe into your abdomen and release the tiny pixel-particles down your legs and out the bottoms of your feet.*

18. *See a spot 6 inches below your feet, between your feet…breathe into that spot… and see the tiny pixel-particles drain down your body, go through the spot, and be absorbed into the earth…see the tiny pixel-particles drain down your body, go through that spot, and be absorbed…absorbed…absorbed into the earth.*

19. *Place your feet flat against the floor. See a six-inch sphere 18 inches beneath your feet. Breathe into the sphere…breathe into the sphere and see the tiny pixel-particles release from the sphere…see the tiny, tiny pixel-particles releasing from the sphere.*

20. *Breathe into your heart…breathe into your heart and release the tiny pixel-particles out your heart…releasing the tiny pixel-particles out of your heart.*

21. *Breathe into the depths of your heart…breathe into the deep, deep depths of your heart, and release the tiny, tiny pixel-particles from the deep depths of your heart… releasing the tiny pixel-particles from the deep depths of your heart.*

22. *Breathe into your throat…breathe into your throat and release the tiny pixel-particles out your throat…releasing the tiny pixel-particles out of your throat.*

23. *Breathe into your voice…breathe into the depths of your voice and release the tiny pixel-particles from your voice…releasing the tiny pixel-particles from the deep depths of your voice.*

24. *Breathe into the right side of your brain…breathe into the right side of your brain and release the tiny, tiny pixel-particles out the right side of your brain…releasing the tiny pixel-particles out the right side of your brain.*

25. *Breathe into the left side of your brain…breathe into the left side of your brain and release the tiny, tiny pixel-particles out the left side of your brain…releasing the tiny pixel-particles out the left side of your brain.*

26. *Breathe into the front of your brain…breathe into the front of your brain and release the tiny, tiny pixel-particles out the front of your brain…releasing the tiny pixel-particles out the front of your brain.*

27. *Breathe into the back of your brain…breathe into the back of your brain and release the tiny, tiny pixel-particles out the back of your brain…releasing the tiny pixel-particles out the back of your brain.*

28. *Breathe into the center of your brain…breathe into the center of your brain and see the tiny, tiny pixel-particles, releasing, radiating out in all directions from the center of your brain…see the tiny pixel-particles, releasing, radiating out in all directions from the center of your brain.*

ImTT Press, publisher

29. *Breathe into your mind...breathe into the deep depths of your mind and release the tiny pixel-particles from your mind...releasing the tiny pixel-particles from the deep depths of your mind.*

30. *Breathe into the core of your self...breathe into what you think of as the core of your self and release the tiny pixel-particles from the core of your self...releasing the tiny pixel-particles from the core of your self.*

31. *Imagine that you are about to yawn. Imagine that you are yawning a deep, wide yawn. As you yawn, see the tiny pixel-particles release from the core of your self...as you feel the yawn throughout your whole body...as you feel the yawn throughout your whole body, see the tiny pixel-particles releasing from the core of your self.*

32. *Scan your body to see if there are any particles remaining in your body. If there are, breathe into that part of your body and then breathe the tiny pixel-particles out the pores of your skin in that area.*

33. *Let's re-evaluate the image. What is your emotional reaction to the image now?*

34. *[At this point, the person's attitude toward the image should have altered. If the person's attitude has not changed, re-evaluate the situation for additional emotions.]*

ImTT Press, publisher

References

Miller, R. M. (2002). *The Dynamics of Food Addiction.* Paper written for Pacific Graduate Institute. Library of Congress. www.fsaprotocol.com

Miller, R. M. (2004). The Feeling-state Theory of Compulsions and Cravings and Decreasing Compulsions and Cravings Using an Eye Movement Protocol. (Doctoral dissertation). Carpinteria, CA: Pacifica Graduate Institute.

Miller, R. M. (2010). The Feeling-State Theory of Impulse-Control Disorders and the Impulse-Control Protocol. *Traumatology, 16(3),* 2-10.

Miller, R. M. (2012). Treatment of Behavioral Addictions Utilizing the Feeling-State Addiction Protocol: A Multiple Baseline Study, *Journal of EMDR Practice and Research, 6(4),* 159-169.

Miller, R. (2015). *Image Transformation Therapy.* Vista, CA: ImTT Press.

Miller, R. (2016). *Image Transformation Therapy Scripts for Therapists.* Vista, CA: ImTT Press.

Shapiro, F. (1995). *Eye movement desensitization and reprocessing: Basic principles, protocols and procedures.* New York, NY: Guilford.

Shapiro, F. (2001). *Eye movement desensitization and reprocessing: Basic principles, protocols and procedures (2nd ed.).* New York, NY: Guilford.

ImTT Press, publisher

ImTT Press, publisher

Glossary of Terms with Acronyms

Assured-Survival Feeling (ASF): ASFs are the result of experiences that promote a person's survival. Examples of ASFs are feelings of belonging, being special, important, loved, or safe.

Bilateral Stimulation (BLS): The processing of a memory using alternating side-to-side stimulation, such as eye movements, sound, or tappers.

Changing Patterns Protocol (CPP): An ImTT protocol used to trigger changes in psychological patterns that were created as a result of a previous dysfunctional image.

Euphoric Sensation Release Protocol (ESRP): The ESRP reduces the intensity of the euphoric or rush sensation of a Sensation-FS.

Eye Movement Desensitization and Reprocessing (EMDR): A psychotherapy shown effective for processing traumatic memories, using BLS.

Feeling-State (FS): A fixated linkage between an ASF and a person, behavior, or object. The FS is postulated to be a cause of both behavioral and substance addictions.

Feeling-State Addiction Protocol (FSAP): The protocol for breaking the fixation of the FS. The FSAP utilizes a modified form of EMDR for processing the FS.

Feeling-State Image Protocol (FSIP): The protocol for breaking the fixation of the FS. The FSIP utilizes the protocols of Image Transformation Therapy for processing the FS.

Feeling-State Theory: The theory that explains how FSs create behavioral and substance addictions.

Feeling-State Therapy (FST): The therapy for processing substance and behavioral addiction based on Feeling-State Theory.

Image: In ImTT, the word "image" is defined as a psychologically powered mental representation. The image could be powered by feelings of pain, terror, ASFs, or culturally accepted images such what is considered "manly."

Image Transformation Therapy (ImTT): A new therapy that utilizes different forms of breathing/visualization protocols to process trauma, OCD, anxiety, shock, depression, and phobias.

Image De-Construction Protocol (IDP): An ImTT protocol that eliminates traumatic or dysfunctional images. ImTT is often used in conjunction with the P/TRP.

Intergenerational Joining: An FS in which the person unconsciously mimics a behavior or quality of another person, often a parent. Using "parent" as an example, the person feels connected with the "parent" by taking on a characteristic of the "parent."

ImTT Press, publisher

Pain/Terror Release Protocol (P/TRP): An ImTT protocol that releases pain and terror in such a way that it is not necessary for the person to experience the feeling in order to process it. ImTT is often used in the processing of trauma.

Positive Feeling Scale (PFS): A zero to 10 scale that measures the intensity of a person's experience of a positive feeling.

Psychologically induced FS: An FS that is created because of an intensified need for an ASF.

Sensation-FS: An FS that is composed entirely of an intensely positive sensation, such as a euphoric high or the Adrenaline excitement triggered by danger.

Books by Robert Miller, PhD

Image Transformation Therapy

Image Transformation Therapy Scripts for Therapists

(available on Amazon)

Training

For information about training workshops and

certification in FSAP or ImTT go to

www.fsaprotocol.com

www.imtherapy.com